A DOZEN IDEA-FILLED CHAPTERS.

BAKIN' IN A CRAVEABLE BRAND

Active Ingredients Enclosed

BAKIN' IN A CRAVEABLE BRAND

KEVIN MOEHLENKAMP

A front-row seat to how companies like Dunkin', Microsoft, and Liberty Mutual become beloved brands.

BRIGHTRAY
PUBLISHING®

We help busy professionals write and publish their stories
to distinguish themselves and their brands.

(407) 287-5700 | Winter Park, FL
info@BrightRay.com | www.BrightRay.com

ISBN: 978-1-956464-44-3

Published in the United States of America.
BrightRay Publishing ® 2023

NOTABLE
PRAISE

"Persuasion is not a numbers game. Great brands make you feel something—love, laughter, tears, joy. Kevin gives us a roadmap back to this.

Gerry Graf, Co-Founder and CCO of SlapGlobal and Business Insider's "Most Creative Man in Advertising"

"At a critical time, Kevin's passion and insights around emotional branding helped secure Microsoft's place as a global tech leader with heart.

Mich Mathews-Spradlin, Former Global CMO of Microsoft

"*Bakin' in a Craveable Brand* is a game changer for all marketers.

Donna Josephson, CMO of Shipley Do-Nuts

"There is a lifetime of world-class experience baked into this excellent book, providing inspiring ideas to help any marketer build meaningful and profitable brand relationships with their customers.

Lesley Bielby, CEO of DiMassimo Goldstein and Author of "Super Strategist"

"The book is a great reminder that the entire organization needs to understand and live the brand. I finished the book motivated to do the work to ensure our brand's continued health.

Michael Morse, President and CEO of Louisiana Fish Fry

"I've had the pleasure of working with Kevin on multiple food and beverage brands. This book is an insightful and engaging read that allows anyone to tap into his keys for successfully developing and nurturing brands.

Melissa Gilreath, VP of Marketing of TruRoots Company

"Moehlenkamp's ability to tap into the emotional core of a brand sets him apart as a thought-leader. A must-read that will leave you energized and ready to transform your brand.

Meagan Price, VP of Marketing of American Family Care

TABLE OF CONTENTS

"This book is dedicated to my amazing wife and four extraordinary children who have patiently suffered through my obsession with branding, marketing, and truly terrible Dad jokes. In a life dedicated to creativity, my family will always be my most proud and beloved creation."

FOREWORD: BRINGING BRAND BACK

A Brand. It's become synonymous with a tagline, a logo, a vision, or a product. Even the marketing industry can't seem to concisely communicate what makes a brand a BRAND! The truth is, a brand is all of those things and more. It isn't a singular thing or campaign: it's an idea. An image. A mission. A unifying belief system that's born from a company's very core and can inform a company's every move. But the unfortunate reality is that, for most companies, a brand is an elusive mirage that they feel exists well beyond their reach. They see it as an unattainable dream for companies that are too small to compete with their larger, better-funded adversaries.

But today, I'll share with you a secret that your well-funded competitors would rather you didn't know: a strong brand that the world craves is within reach for companies of all sizes and resources. All they need is the clarity and courage to pursue it. It is the intention of this book to provide clarity if you are willing to bring the courage. Despite what you may believe, brands are not elusive creatures that mysteriously appear from the marketing brand-o-sphere. Brands are thoughtfully made and lovingly nourished in the same way a cabinet maker puts on his apron and methodically gets on with "making" cabinets. There are simple steps that, when followed, will deliver to anyone a brand that transforms every aspect of their company and slays their goliaths. And that idea may perhaps be the most important idea you could take from this book and it's worth repeating. The world's most successful businesses bake brand into every aspect of their companies.

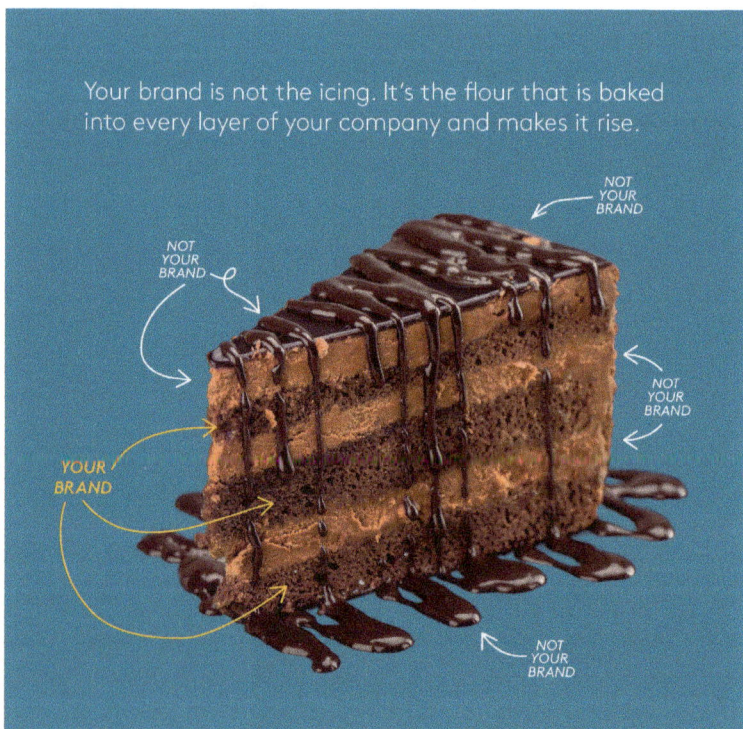

Your brand is not the icing. It's the flour that is baked into every layer of your company and makes it rise.

NOT YOUR BRAND

NOT YOUR BRAND

NOT YOUR BRAND

YOUR BRAND

NOT YOUR BRAND

A brand is often diminished to elements of advertising. Think of frosting: pretty to look at, it tastes good, but very few people would buy an entire plate of it.

This is your advertising—the smart, colorful, and catchy outward communication of your brand to the world. But your brand must go much deeper than that to drive the success you are looking for. It needs to exist in every layer of your company. It's the flour that supports the very foundation of your cake, which is your company. Without flour, your cake would be a big flop. It's the same for a company that wrongfully believes a brand only lives in its colorful window dressings and tries to operate without its brand baked into everything.

Every move a company makes should exude and extend its unique brand story. The great brand prognosticator Simon Sinek understood this brand truth and distilled it into a simple, game-changing proclamation: "People don't buy *what* you do; they buy *why* you do it."[1] But even with the introduction of Simon Sinek's timeless marketing epiphany, a lot of questions continue to swirl around what a brand is and why anyone needs one. Questions like:

- What is a brand composed of?
- Is it the domain of only large companies?
- Is branding different from marketing?
- Can a strong brand really make a company grow?
- Does my company have what it takes?

If you're reading this book, you're likely asking yourself one or more of these questions. You're wondering if your business could benefit from branding and if you're ready to start developing your brand right now. The prospect can be intimidating and it's not always clear where to begin. Maybe you're not even sure what the process of branding your business would entail, or even what branding *is*.

I hope this book will act as a simple and informative starting point for the thousands of businesses that are still searching for their brands or who are hesitant to even begin the search. I'll show you that not only *can* companies of any size build a great brand, but they *have to* brand. The good news is, I'm confident that you and your company already have the tools you need to build your brand right now. From there, it's a simple matter of obtaining a roadmap to successfully navigate your brand journey. This book is that roadmap.

Branding isn't a random instance of pixie dust with unrepeatable magic. There are proven steps to take, deep questions to ask yourself, and you'll need the courage to abide by your brand once it's born—and it's all within your reach.

You may be asking yourself, who is this ad guy who dares to make such bold declarations? If I sound overly confident in my mastery of branding, it's simply because I have created, or been a part of creating, iconic brands for hundreds of some of the most well-known companies in the world and for other companies that were too small for you to have ever heard of—each one has watched their business transform just the same. All of those companies, whether they were Microsoft, FedEx, Dunkin', Visa, or Bristol Seafoods (a small New England seafood purveyor) informed my approach to building timeless brands. From those experiences, I have learned what works and, perhaps more importantly, what doesn't work when it comes to transformative brand building. Maybe the most important branding lesson I learned from all of my years was that branding is not the sole domain of well-funded mega-corporate behemoths. It is there for the taking for anyone bold enough to act and commit. The benefits for all of these courageous companies, whether they be large or small, are exponential. As an example, let's look at one of those companies I had the privilege of creating a craveable brand for, Dunkin' Donuts.

Today, Dunkin' Donuts is a coffee and donuts giant. It has 12,000 stores in 45 countries, and according to the most recent data, it serves 1.9 billion cups of coffee a year.[2] It's a household name, and its products can be found not just in their cafes, but in grocery stores across the country. However, this wasn't always the case. Few remember that Dunkin' Donuts started out as a small but popular coffee shop in Quincy, Massachusetts in the 1940s. It grew into a chain over time, with locations spread across the Boston area. Dunkin' was well positioned with its business model to expand quickly, but it also faced large headwinds. Namely, a formidable coffee powerhouse with an odd mermaid logo was spreading eastward from Seattle. As its store counts grew, Dunkin' was beginning to look beyond its New England roots and was putting itself directly on a cross-country collision course with Starbucks. Born from Seattle's established coffee culture, Starbucks already had a strong reputation for "fancy gourmet coffee" for the coffee elite. Dunkin' desperately needed a way to differentiate itself from Starbucks if it hoped to have any chance of not being driven out of its cozy New England town.

About the time this tempest in a coffee pot was brewing, I entered Dunkin's orbit in 2004. Dunkin' Donuts was determined to go head-to-head with the Seattle coffee chain but on what grounds? My amazingly talented team and I knew that to pull this off, we couldn't out-maneuver Starbucks by trying to be another Starbucks. Yes, Dunkin' has great coffee, but its coffee quality story doesn't hold a candle to Starbucks. We had to offer the world an alternative story, one that was true to its brand, true to its customers, and one that would champion and energize a whole new universe of consumers.

We presented our branding campaign in a flurry of insightful, creative, thoroughly-researched brand applications, and irrefutable proofs of the benefits of branding. Our plan was pinned to the walls and written across the table. We didn't limit it to a new slogan or a few pieces of promotional artwork. We planned to reconfigure the entire company's image. Dunkin' Donuts was no Starbucks. It wasn't for gourmands spending hours in cafes with their laptops. This was a coffee shop for blue-collar workers; the people who get up before dawn, who build our roads, our power lines, and our water mains. They didn't have time to luxuriate in a latte shop and Dunkin' proudly knew it. Our entire campaign relied on this distinction, and connecting it all together was this simple yet powerful brand message: "America Runs on Dunkin'."

Those four simple words acknowledged and celebrated the importance of the hard-working people who are the backbone of our country, while subtly (or not-so-subtly) de-positioning the luxuriating Starbucks loyalists. But we still weren't sure if the top brass would bite. There's often a dissonance between creatives and the people who sign the marketing checks—we believed in the brand, but had we convinced *them*? Spoiler alert: we had.

By 2006, our "America Runs on Dunkin'" campaign rolled out, and we pulled off one of the biggest David and Goliath stories in marketing history. Dunkin' Donuts, the humble, East Coast coffee franchise, had successfully challenged Starbucks. And instead of being overshadowed by the Seattle powerhouse—as so many other coffee chains had, like Peet's Coffee, Seattle's Best, and Tully's—Dunkin' Donuts came out bigger and better than ever. It didn't try to mimic the success of Starbucks and instead created its own, Craveable Brand (more about that later). Starbucks left a gap in the marketplace, one where a busy worker who doesn't have the luxury of waiting for their much-needed morning coffee fix could get their needs met quickly. They just wanted a good, quick cup of coffee to fuel their day at work. Dunkin' Donuts was able to provide that fresh perspective in a way that creatively recognized and celebrated their crucial contributions as engines of the American dream. *This* is the powerful lift that true branding can bring to challenger brands like Dunkin'; that can make all the difference.

One of our first and perhaps most telegraphic ads we created to introduce America Runs on Dunkin' to the world.[3]

But branding is much more than a catchy slogan. The magic of branding happens in the "magic middle" where creativity tangos with business and cultural insights and each side lifts the other to new heights. As a set of four words strung together, "America Runs on Dunkin'" isn't really all that clever. It's the business insight and emotional resonance that is unlocked by those words that make them so special and iconic.

When we approached the Dunkin' Donuts executives, we didn't just bring them an advertising campaign they were expecting. Our plan hinged on changing the entire company's image, both in the public eye and in the eyes of its employees and leaders. We not only had to enfold them in a new brand image that customers would fall in love with but one that Dunkin' would fall in love with as well. Top to bottom. It takes love to create the enthusiasm necessary for a company to completely re-imagine itself. To build a successful brand, we weren't just asking them to buy a marketing idea, we were asking them to commit their entire organization to a bold new mission and vision.

"America Runs on Dunkin'" is bigger than coffee or donuts; it's a platform built on an intrinsically human idea: the working class is the backbone of any society. They quietly keep America running without much recognition, and Dunkin' promised to see them and to keep *them* running. It's an almost romantic notion, this promise of the official coffee provider of the over-worked and under-recognized. And that's exactly why it worked. We took a tiny Boston franchise and put it on the global market by revamping its business culture and simplifying its message. This is why branding is so important, especially for challenger companies. If you want to compete with the Goliaths of your industry, your company needs a compelling, clear message to rally behind. One that stirs emotions and elicits irrational loyalty. You may think you're not big enough or powerful enough to brand your company, but that couldn't be further from the truth. At its core, every company has a strong brand yearning to be released, and this book can show you how to unearth, define, and set yours free.

Although my experience working with Dunkin' is a good example of the impact of proper branding, it wasn't an isolated incident. I've worked in the branding and advertising world for decades, and I have been lucky to be in the driver's seat of countless brands, creating and watching the exponential growth power of branding. I've been in the role of Chief Creative Officer for marketing agencies all across the country, and some brands I've had the honor of shaping include industry icons like FedEx, Visa, HBO, and Microsoft. And while I've had my fair share of success stories, many of those brand victories were hard-fought. My feet have been held to the fire in many a conference room as I sought to elevate a company's brand to propel its growth. I've stared down the barrel of a scarlet-faced Steve Balmer—former CEO of Microsoft—as he spat out, "This better work or I'll fire your whole company." High stakes, but luckily the transformative power of branding once again worked its magic, and Microsoft was spared the debilitating blow of being broken up as a monopoly by the U.S. Department of Justice. I've built successful brands for companies in different industries and at every stage of their growth, from the world's largest supplier of plasma cutters to the world's largest toy manufacturer, and right down to a humble chainsaw carver from the outskirts of Maine. Their brand stories are the stories of my life. And every one of those experiences helped shape and hone my agency's approach to building not just ordinary brands but brands that customers yearn for. We call them Craveable Brands.

Over three decades as a franchise business owner, marketing consultant, and award-winning creative director and CEO, I've developed a cohesive, streamlined branding process so that companies of any size can:

- Mine the analytical insights needed to discover and nurture a great brand;
- Develop the necessary creative processes to craft a differentiated, emotional storyline behind every beloved brand;
- Articulate a brand platform so that it will serve every aspect of a company from marketing communications right down to employee recruitment.

From established companies looking to pivot to challenger businesses looking for exponential growth, I've helped develop brand platforms for almost every conceivable type of company. Whether they've been in their industry for decades or they're just getting started, I've helped these challenger brands compete, and often surpass, their largest competitors.

You may think your business isn't big or powerful enough to develop a brand—many people do. But that's simply not the case. Anyone can (and should) brand. The price of entry is not nearly as daunting as you have been led to believe. If you have a business, you should have a brand—I cannot say that emphatically enough.

I've survived the slings and arrows of a fickle industry long enough to witness firsthand how powerful branding can be . . . when it's executed correctly. Executives and financiers are often nervous when taking a chance on a creative venture, even when the data shows it's worthwhile. Dunkin' Donuts had to make a decision as a challenger company to simply say "yes" to becoming a brand and then take the steps to fearlessly align its whole company around it.

So why aren't more companies branding? It's my feeling that our industry has made the joyful journey of brand-building seem much more mysterious and daunting than it is. In reality, it's the process of creating a distinctive, compelling, and long-lasting image in the market—succinctly put, it's shaping a brand's customer perception and reputation.

The unvarnished truth is that brands are equal parts brilliant insight, creativity, and commitment. I'm not saying it's easy to develop a successful brand. It's *a lot* of hard work! But while branding is an often difficult endeavor, there's nothing mysterious or inaccessible about it. It's a straightforward process: find the core of your business and make that your brand. "America Runs on Dunkin'" isn't some grand statement. It doesn't make outlandish promises, or even promote donuts and coffee. It's a simple and effective message mined from insights through laser-focused observation. And while it may seem like an intimidating endeavor, it's always worth the effort to develop a strong brand. It has the power to take your business from a product or service to something more powerful: an idea. A mission. A promise.

Nike doesn't just sell sportswear; it sells inspiration and encouragement to athletes of all colors, shapes, and sizes: "Just do it." When people buy their shoes, they're buying that idea. That's the difference branding can make for you too. You can become more than simply a product or service. You can become a way of being to your customers. And when you do, you will become indispensable to them.

With these pages, you can gain confidence and arm yourself with the tools to accomplish what Dunkin', Microsoft, Chili's, and so many others have attained: baking brand greatness into all that you do.

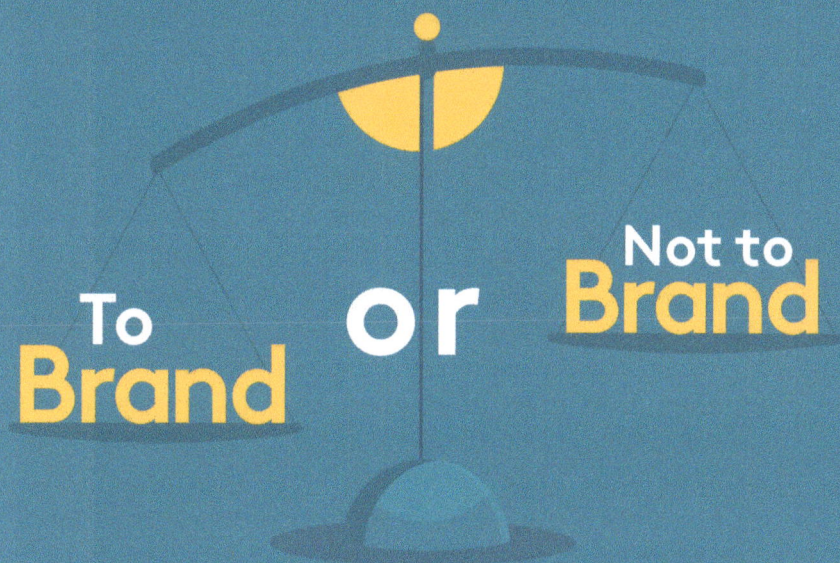

Chapter one

To Brand **or** Not to Brand

Before we get started on how any company *can* brand, it's probably not a bad idea to first explore whether you even believe your company *should* brand. To brand or not to brand is a rhetorical question at this point. The rise of internet transparency, ever-increasing messaging pollution, increased competition, and consumers now sitting squarely in the driver's seat have all left companies with no other option than to brand. But given all of these changing conditions, it has never been harder in the history of time to differentiate your company and stand out in the minds of your target audience. So how then does a company differentiate itself? The answer lies squarely at the heart of your company. And it is proven in study after study.

With current market conditions putting more constraints on how a company can innovate and differentiate itself from its competitors, companies will need to shift their thinking and look inside their walls at their *culture and beliefs* to create the type of innovation they need to differentiate and succeed. I first came across this timely insight in a Harvard Business Review article authored by Douglas Holt. In his article, Holt posited that companies today are faced with the need to innovate or die. But when companies think of innovation, they traditionally jump to product innovation as their sole path to growth. However, product innovation is probably the easiest thing for your competitors to replicate. Look at the growing manufacturing prowess of China and its global dominance in making products faster and cheaper. So if product innovation can no longer be relied upon to drive differentiation and sustainable growth, how will companies innovate? Holt introduced a more evergreen approach to innovation that isn't so easily duplicated called Cultural Innovation—the idea of repositioning a company to focus on its unique values and perspective instead of solely on its products, which demands a constant state of one-up-manship with competitors.[1]

Directing your energy towards one-upping your competitors is akin to burning money; they aren't your target audience, so instead of trying to outpace them, focus on out-branding them by deeply understanding the emotional needs of your consumers and then demonstrating *why* you are *the* company uniquely positioned to understand and satisfy those needs.

So if product innovation is no longer the reliable means to sustainable growth that it once was, certainly spending loads of money on product advertising is tantamount to rearranging deck chairs on the Titanic. And if Cultural Innovation is the new Product Innovation, what then is the evolution of product advertising? You guessed it: Brand Innovation. To me, "Brand Innovation" is the next frontier in turning what, until now, you may have considered your company's softest assets into your hardest and most compelling assets. It's the next step in creatively and convincingly articulating your Cultural Innovation and sharing it with the world. Not just as another company offering, but as *the* company offering. An offering that, when properly captured and expressed, can never be duplicated and pressed out on an assembly line in China.

You're playing a different game now—one where your competitors can't even oppose you.[1] Cultural Innovation fits hand in glove with Brand Innovation. When you articulate your true culture, it will have the power to inspire and form your brand and give new meaning to how you go to market as a company. With this, you've made your business irreplaceable and untouchable.

Consider the top 100 Fortune 500 companies: the best ones have memorable brands that "evoke positive sentiments, epitomized by the brand logo" and stand out from their competitors. You can only evoke that sentiment through accessible, consistent, and instantly recognizable communication.[2] Reflect on the brands below:[3]

- State Farm Insurance: "Like a good neighbor, State Farm is there."
- Nike: "Just do it."
- Subway: "Eat fresh."
- Mastercard: "Priceless."

Four different industries, four different messages, and yet, there's a similarity between these examples: each of these brands embodies more than their logo, tagline, or product. They embody an ideal. And beyond that, they've taken a corner of the market and claimed it. Try as Adidas might, it can't replace Nike as the go-to brand for athletes, no matter how many new product launches it has. Nor can any other competitor, near or far, in the athletic apparel industry.

As a challenger brand, you can't aspire to reach this brand recognition overnight. However, you *can* make the decision to begin this journey today. Actively engage with your target audience now and you'll see an instant positive impact. Defining and publicly establishing your company's brand can significantly influence the success and longevity of your company.

Marketing, Advertising, and Branding: Which Is Which?

To brand or not to brand may be a question that many people aren't even in a position to properly answer. Due to the confusion around the myriad definitions of brand, many people believe they are creating their brand when, in actuality, they are creating something different or far less valuable. People in our industry commonly use words like marketing, advertising, and branding interchangeably. But to use them synonymously reduces the strength of each one and muddies the waters for clients and agencies alike.

Each of these elements is distinct and pursues different goals. You always need to start with defining your brand first—how can you go on to marketing and advertising if you're unsure of what experience you're selling? That's right, you can't. Many businesses try to skip the branding step or, worse yet, diminish branding as a tagline marketing tactic. Branding must be at the core of your marketing and advertising strategies and is therefore the first logical step to define your business.

As we venture forth in our discussion of whether you should brand, it is probably a good time to clarify the basic, but very important, differences in these industry terms so your best efforts are in service of the job at hand. To clarify further:[4]

Clarifying a Muddled Industry

Let's start with some definitions

brand•ing:

At the most basic level, **"branding"** is made up of a company's:

LOGO | MISSION | VISUAL DESIGN | TONE OF VOICE

mar•ket•ing:

Marketing is the process of reaching the target audience and addressing their needs, wants, and fears. It focuses on market-fit and making those Sales.

ad•ver•tis•ing:

Advertising is a marketing strategy used to raise awareness of your brand, business, and products/services.

Brand\\ build•ing:

Brand building is the process of creating a distinctive, compelling and long-lasting image in the market, shaping a brand's customer perception and reputation.

Lead with Brand or Be Led Astray

Quite often, companies who choose not to brand (and therefore never see the ROI of strategic brand practices) exhibit many of the same bad habits. Most of the time, you can look to leadership for a company's failure to brand itself. If there's a lack of strong leadership, which results in a lack of commitment to the brand's message, then it's unrealistic to think that the rest of the company could effectively embrace the brand. There's an old saying: you can't put the cart before the horse and expect it to go where you want. Of course not. How can the horse even see where it's going if its view is constantly blocked by the cart in front of it? You can't expect a company's day-to-day business initiatives, a.k.a the carts, to provide the vision and direction that takes you where you need to go.

Your vision must always lead you. With your vision leading the way, you can not only guide the cart in the right direction, but you can also easily hitch up endless carts behind it. They will miraculously fall neatly in line right behind the brand vision you put at the front. Now imagine all those carts hitched up end-to-end and being pushed from behind. They will push each other out of line willy-nilly, wreaking havoc and blocking the way forward. But that is exactly how most companies are trying to drive their businesses forward.

Companies that attempt to lead with their initiatives (products, R&D, budgets, etc.) in front of their brand are wasting too much energy herding carts from behind. Now don't get me wrong, business initiatives are an important part of your business plan, but if you're looking for consistent, sustainable, efficient, and meaningful growth, you'll need to have the courage to look inward and put your brand out in front of all else.

That is precisely where Dunkin' was stuck when I took over as Chief Creative Officer for its marketing agency. For some time, it had been herding together the year's menu initiatives, and then marching them out under the banner of another tagline du jour. It didn't take long for me to see that the deep customer love for this brand went way beyond the need for another cup of coffee or a new snack offering. I knew there was a Brand with a capital B hiding in plain sight, dying to be uncovered and articulated.

I saw it written on the faces of all of those hard-working customers lined up for their daily dose of "put me in coach." Getting Dunkin' to see the potential was the tricky part though. In order to get them to break from the familiar comfort of "marketing as usual," we had to strike an out-of-the-ordinary deal.

We got the Dunkin' brass to agree to sit through a five-hour meeting where we would unveil a completely new campaign that was driven by a new brand, not a new product. Five hours for executives is like three days for the average person; executives *don't* like to waste their time. In exchange for the meeting, we agreed that if they didn't buy our big brand idea, our agency would eat the costs associated with developing the presentation— there was no risk and no cost to Dunkin' other than the executives' time. But if they bought the idea, they had to buy this new brand idea as is. That was how confident I was that a hibernating brand was waiting to come out of the cave. Unbeknownst to me, there was more riding on this presentation than the usual high expectations.

With all four walls of our largest conference room covered in customer research and cultural insights, an exhaustive articulation of the proposed brand, and 250 original pieces, "America Runs on Dunkin" came to life before their eyes. Our lead strategist at the time, Justin, gave brilliantly insightful context for what they would see, and our creative team led by Tim Cawley and Tim Foley brought it home. As the CEO got up to leave after having just green-lighted the campaign, he turned to me and said, "I don't know if anyone here shared this with you, Kevin, but when I came in here this morning your agency already had two strikes against it; if this failed, it would have been the third strike. Instead, your team has hit a home run." Indeed, no one bothered to share that small bit of information with me! But the high stakes didn't matter. That day, we helped a good company become a great brand.

Don't Succumb to Trends

Like so many modern companies, before they found their true brand, Dunkin' was stuck in a cycle of product innovation rather than delving deeper into what it was really making. Dunkin' was so consumed with chasing after what its competitors were doing that it never got to the heart of the *why*. It was pumping out a never-ending cycle of product initiatives, but Dunkin' wasn't mining its values to get to what was at the heart of its brand. Once Dunkin' and its customers' values were put at the front of the cart, "America Runs on Dunkin'" was born, and almost two decades later, the name printed on the outside of its coffee cup is worth far more to its customers and their valuation than the hot liquid inside of it. If the Dunkin' executives hadn't agreed to that meeting and said yes to their brand, we're left to wonder if Dunkin' would have been just one more casualty of our trending "better for you" food culture. When faced with whether to brand or not to brand, Dunkin' grabbed the opportunity and ran with it. It hasn't looked back.

The Underestimated Business Tool

Hopefully, at this point, you are starting to believe that no matter which industry you're in, you need to say "yes" to your brand. Companies that think they can skate by on improved product specs or customer service scores alone are missing out on one of the most powerful business tools available to them.

If you look around, you'll see that the competitive landscape has only gotten more vast, and building a brand has become non-negotiable. Some companies inadvertently isolate customers by loading their ads, brochures, and communications with endless industry jargon. This is a major faux pas; don't focus on the features of your product. Instead, highlight your company's larger promise to your customers and industry, and then show how your products fulfill that promise to them. Get specific about your values and core beliefs. Make your company more than "just another product-pusher." Any competitor can copy your business plan and product mix, and in doing so, it will probably do it faster and cheaper. Effective branding may be a company's most powerful business tool to protect itself from an increasingly competitive marketplace.

Company leaders are starting to learn that unless they've inherited an already established brand, such as McDonald's or Disney, they need to intentionally articulate their brand message at every touch point of their company, internally and externally.

People in charge of the budget, the CFOs and CMOs, have historically viewed marketing as a kind of necessary evil. John Wanamaker is known for his famous quote: "Half my advertising spending is wasted; the trouble is I don't know which half."

When I drop this line in a client meeting, it never fails to get a laugh. It resonates with the fear and uncertainty that many clients feel when they're faced with marketing decisions. I try to help clients overcome this baseless fear but sometimes, there's a dissonance. Many individuals in these positions are often data-driven and find comfort in the reliability of facts and figures. What they secretly wish is that all of the marketing could just be a rational, logical, and numbers-based exercise minus all of the creativity and emotional stuff. Sadly, for many companies, that desire can and usually does become a self-fulfilling prophecy. They drink from the firehose of data to the point where the new, not-so-funny marketing adage becomes "I now know that all my marketing budget is working, but it's not driving growth anymore."

Unlike any other time in our history, we have unlimited and immediate access to data and research, so if they wish, a client never has to guess which half of their advertising is working. They have created a perfect CYA scenario for themselves. There are countless agencies that will charge you large sums of money to fill a swimming pool with safe, comforting data that lets you sleep at night. If you visit most marketing agency sites and look at their case studies, many will talk about their commitment to KPIs (Key Performance Indicators) based on online data metrics like increase in click-through rates, conversion rates, etc. (FYI, if you ask most research teams what their recent study shows, they will likely answer "What would you like it to show?") While these metrics may be a calming salve in an unpredictable market environment, they can undermine the true impact of what a great branding effort can do for a company. Don't create the Julia Child of brands only to deploy it as a fry cook. Build your brand to do big things and then shepherd it along to do them. There are no great leaps without some risk and patience.

Brand connections are built over time and yet, some clients demand immediate results. Brand-building success is driven by a continual effort that compounds exponentially over time. It's like dieting: someone has to adopt a lifestyle of healthy eating, not a 2–week fad diet, if they want to see sustainable results. In the same way, you can drop a quick five pounds but gain them back, flashy marketing tactics may garner short-term satisfaction with marginal metric spikes, but they won't translate into sustained sales and long-term loyalty.

Appreciate the harmony between brand-building & sales activation

The 60:40 rule, introduced by Binet and Fields in 2013, is a lighthouse for marketers when allocating spend. It's all about the long and the short of it working together to achieve growth.

Brand Building + Sales Activation

The 60:40 rule has not changed

Brand Building Channels
Brand Building is lasting, emotion, mass awareness – delivers on both long-term and short-term growth/sales.

Sales Activation Channels
Sales Activation is targeted, often measurable, rational, product messaging – delivers only on short-term sales.

% Spend: 100, 90, 80, 70, 60, 50, 40, 30, 20, 10, 0

2000, 2001, 2002, 2002, 2004, 2005, 2006, 2007, 2008, 2009, 2010, 2011

https://www.marketingweek.com/ritson-brand-building-boost-short-term-sales/

It often just takes one stalwart visionary on the leadership team to "buy into" a brand idea and commit to the long-term work necessary to see results. Without this resolve, we see clients go through the preliminary work of branding, stick their insights and values into a catchy tagline, and call it a day. I'll make this clear now: a brand platform is *not* a tagline. Feigning the steps of the process will not make it transformative. Customers have a highly-tuned BS detector now; they know if your brand is authentic and meaningful to them, or if your efforts are insincere. And woe to the companies who don't grasp that difference. A tagline isn't strong enough by itself to win over the hearts and minds of your customers. It's simply the north star that constantly points your company in the right direction of authentically expressing your brand. Your company may get some initial attention for declaring its new brand direction, but it will only be adored and beloved when it lives that brand out in the world every day for all your customers, partners, employees, and family to see.

When companies struggle to get a handle on their brand, I often quote the great advertising legend, George Lois, when he yelled, "The problem is the problem!" at our college VC class.

Companies shouldn't ask "Do we have the right creative? Or the right media plan? Or the right product mix?" No, the question they need to be asking themselves first is, "Have we created a brand that will amplify all of our company's efforts and drive measurable growth?" When they begin by solving that problem first, the answer will help make all of those other questions far easier to answer.

Company leadership can get hung up on the black-and-white details here. It's not about choosing between whether to feature the brand *versus* the product/company; it's about encapsulating the product and company *in* the brand."But what if my company just spent big money producing a new marketing campaign?" you might ask yourself. You don't need to throw out everything you've done to start layering in your brand. You may just need to re-focus that existing marketing around your new, underlying brand message. Be flexible and use creativity to pivot to your new brand.

Through the years, if you were to ask anyone who's ever worked for me or with me, they'll say that I always circle back to the idea that creativity is a business tool. I believe one of the greatest joys of being in marketing isn't simply creating campaign ideas. Although creating award-winning marketing campaigns has been one of the great joys of my life, my real passion is the creative challenge of thoroughly understanding my clients' business needs and narrowing down the opportunity so finely that it almost seems impossible to thread a creative idea through that needle. *That* is when I have set myself a worthy goal as a creative problem solver. That is when you have to be your most creative. That is when you know you are doing something few others can do.

We have to take a random, spontaneous idea on paper to a brilliant, one-of-a-kind solution for clients to apply to a seemingly insurmountable business problem. *That's* the distinct opportunity we get as marketers, making our work unlike any other job in the world.

Anyone can be a brand. And in this modern world, every company out there *must* create a sustainable brand with the possibility for long-term growth if it wants to remain in the game. So to answer the question that begins this chapter: YES. You most definitely need a brand.

Chapter **two**

~~Brand:~~ The Giant Killer

If you're not moving, you're dying. It's true of sharks, and the same can be said for challenger brands. The competitive nature of today's marketplace doesn't allow brands to survive if they meekly aspire to tread water and stay the same size. Successful companies have to constantly be hunting, growing, and learning to survive. Personally, I'm most excited when I'm working with small to mid-sized companies. I like that they take chances and swing for the fences to reach the next level. I also know that, at this crucial stage of their growth, there's an exponential impact branding can have on their drive to get to the top of the heap.

Unfortunately, most companies of this size don't realize how accessible branding is to them. That was reason alone to write this book. It's a rallying cry to all those companies without giant marketing departments and budgets. It's a blueprint laying out the steps that even the most novice marketers can follow to disrupt their category.

Challenger brands are often dismissed as inconsequential, the meek siblings of big, established brands. In reality, challenger brands outnumber the big multinational brands. Boston Consulting Group reported a $20 billion shift in 2017 from big brands to challenger brands, with a similar trend in European markets. Adweek described this market shift to challenger brands as a "global megatrend."[1] Despite this, individual challenger companies can't challenge or displace giant companies *without* branding. In fact, in the battle for market share between category leaders or mid-market and startup businesses, a brand can be a great equalizer. A brand has the power to actually tip the momentum scale in the favor of smaller companies.

Even your largest competitors were challenger brands once too. Original DD in Quincy, Massachusetts.[2]

Take the classic marketing case study of AVIS vs. Hertz. AVIS knew it would be practically impossible to bump Hertz out of the top spot for car rentals by doing the same old thing. So it decided to take what was a market disadvantage and turn it into an advantage. AVIS proudly embraced its challenger status behind the category leader and turned it into a mission that resonated with customers: Avis proudly stated to the country, "Yes, we may be #2 at this moment, but at Avis, that means *we try harder.*" "We try harder!" even made it onto lapel buttons throughout 300 cities to reinforce Avis' commitment to its customers.[3]

Instead of seeing its competitor's dominance as a deterrent, AVIS leveraged it by creating a more honest brand that consumers could rally behind. Challengers may trail behind multinational companies, but they are committed to working twice as hard because of it. And customers love this notion. Who doesn't want to root for an underdog?

Challenger brands may not aim to become a big brand, but they still need to be hungry for growth. The advantage that comes with challenger brands is that they have the opportunity of a fresh slate. While your large competitor may very likely be living with an outdated or poorly constructed brand, you can build a more modern and compelling brand from the ground up. Without the confinements of an already-established brand, which comes with existing expectations and handcuffs, you have room for brand innovation to take risks and give consumers what they have been craving. A brand is a great place to stake your claim in the market. Consumers aren't necessarily looking for a replacement product, but they are always open to something new to believe in.

Consider Liquid Death. At first glance, the black can is sleek, made edgy with the gold skull embossed in the center. It's a surprise to learn that Liquid Death isn't beer, hard liquor, or an energy drink: it's water. Water is a necessity and there are countless brands touting the same benefits and employing the same marketing tactics. But newcomer Liquid Death came in, identified a new corner of the market, and created a new approach to hydrating.

Other bottled water companies focus on a refreshing or natural aesthetic, but Liquid Death broke the category rules and went in a completely new direction. Unlike other industries with countless innovations, the food and beverage industries have some limitations. There are only so many ways to reformulate and repackage foods and drinks. You don't exactly hear of food "inventions," so the key lies with the branding. Liquid Death accomplished this by creating luxury water with a punk aesthetic. Why not?! A challenger's worst mistake is believing success lies in emulating.

If branding is a good tactic for established brands, it's a *great* one for challenger brands. It's very effective at keeping the ship upright, meaning a brand is the wind in your sails. To keep your course true, it needs to connect to the core of your business. Brands sustain established companies, but for challenger brands, they're rocket fuel. Branding can help answer the question: "How can I not only survive my competitors but eliminate them?" As we mentioned, people love to root for the dark horse almost as much as they like to witness the fall of the mighty. It's tough in some ways to be an established brand, because people expect you to eventually succumb to an underdog, and they're ready to cheer for those challenger brands. Take Menards. Unless you live in the Midwest, you may not have heard of this comparatively small hardware chain. Despite only operating in fourteen states, it is the #3 home improvement store in America. RetailWire called Menards "the most customer-centric DIY-brand."[4] Because of their dedication to customer experience, creative pricing, and an incredibly robust rebate program, Menards has risen through the ranks to contend with home improvement giants like Home Depot and Lowe's. Their customers are fiercely loyal and report not only an improved shopping experience, but also higher quality items and service, and it's all thanks to branding! Menards looked at the competition and set themselves apart by identifying a gap in the market.

There are some telltale signs that mark when a challenger brand is starting to make big moves against its larger competitors. It begins with a social buzz; customers start noticing and celebrating the challenger brand. They "switch allegiances" and become brand ambassadors. At this stage, customers are no longer happy to sit on the sidelines as passive consumers; they are up and advocating for your company.

It's these regular people, not the well-paid influencers, who will ultimately stoke the winds of change and set the challenger brand on its new trajectory. And why would these regular people do such a thing for a company?

Hint: It's not because the product or service is that much better than everyone else's. It's because these consumers believe in what the company stands for. They believe in its brand and the products that support it. People don't advocate for a bar of soap, but they *will* advocate for a company such as Dove because it advocates for a world where "Real Beauty" is recognized and celebrated. Give your customers something to believe in and fight for and you'll be irreplaceable.

Some companies have achieved enviable growth without a well-defined brand. Some large companies have amassed a large customer following before they got their brand right. But these are exceptions. And usually, it catches up to them.

Google is one of these rare companies that found success early on without a brand to guide them. It built a technology that changed the world. In its early days, Google was originally thought of simply as a tool for acquiring information. A d*mn good tool to be certain, but the tool didn't capture our hearts as much as our minds. Now Google represents so much more than a search engine. It offers a suite of services, like Gmail, Google Calendar, and Google Groups, and it has built these services around a core idea: "to organize the world's information and make it universally accessible and useful."[5] Today, its brand is reflected across all of its marketing platforms. Google brilliantly expresses its value as more than just a tool. It is an enabler of human connection. Now that's a belief we can get behind, right?

Another great example of companies that led with a product and followed with a brand is Uber and Lyft. Modern taxis have been around since the 19th century, but these rideshare companies came in and offered something new: a more personalized riding experience that took advantage of modern technology. According to the New York Times, Uber rides have surpassed taxi rides and there's little indication that Uber and Lyft will take the back seat anytime soon. They'd amassed a large customer base before the brand came around.[6] So if you're creating the next world-changing technology like Google or Lyft, sure, you might just be able to successfully build your company without a brand for a short time. But that's a big "if." Those are some mighty big shoes to fill when it comes to product innovation, and it's more likely you will need to create a compelling brand from the start to achieve anything close to their meteoric success.

Creating a potent challenger brand means understanding why companies do what they do and why they believe in their products. It's touchy-feely stuff, stuff that isn't readily apparent in your research and data. You're going to have to get comfortable with feeling uncomfortable. It can feel risky going all-in on establishing your brand, particularly if the creative approach feels out of your comfort zone. Companies often worry that their employees and target customers will get some sort of "culture shock" when they buy into this new brand when, in most cases, it is their own uneasiness being projected onto others. Allow me to allay your worries: by making your brand authentic to who you are, there shouldn't be much of a transition. If you do the work and truly uncover your core values, you don't have to worry about it feeling different or inauthentic because the core attributes of your company are what your brand is built on. It's what makes you unique, sets you apart from competitors, and prepares you to challenge your industry leaders. Believe me, your employees and customers will thank you, not question you.

This was reinforced in my mind when I worked with Liberty Mutual to define its brand and marketing. Think of it: insurance is often dismissed as the driest of consumer offerings. Just look at how Geico and Progressive address their customer base to liven up a dry life necessity—a funny gecko and bubbly Flo. These campaigns are iconic and unrepeatable to their competitors.

Liberty needed to find its connection to customers through its authentic values. Geico was hammering away to establish itself as the low-cost provider, with "15 minutes will save you 15 percent," while Liberty Mutual actually had larger premiums. However, it cost more because it invested more in customer service and accepted responsibility for servicing their customers. So how does reliability go head-to-head with an adorable gecko?

"Responsibility. What's Your Policy?" Our newly proposed brand platform written by Ernie Schenk, another great creative brand zealot who worked for me at the time, started a movement around the world that prompted taking responsibility for our actions and doing the right thing. This is what Liberty Mutual strived for every day, and we built its successful new brand based on what it already was and asked like-minded people around the world to join it in its mission. Liberty Mutual has its responsibility mission literally carved in large type on the walls of its lobby. Don't get me wrong, I love Geico commercials. I just aspire to build brands for companies that have more to give back to the world than talking creatures.

Liberty Mutual would have never made it onto the map if it'd launched a Geico or Progressive approach; it would always have been seen as a desperate copycat, a poor imitation of the wacky originals that customers would instantly see through. Instead, Liberty Mutual found a new approach and incorporated that identity into its brand. *That's* what made it compelling: Liberty Mutual differentiated itself from its competition instead of chasing market share by emulating the category leaders and hoping for their table scraps. As a disappointing side note, Liberty Mutual has recently abandoned its authentic brand and is now firmly in the camp of insurance spokespersons (or spokes-animal I guess you'd say)—an emu to be exact.

As a challenger brand, a crucial question in the brand excavation process must be answered: who's in the driver's seat and calling the shots for your company? And can you make them your biggest brand advocate? A challenger brand can't dream of becoming more without unanimous support. CEOs, CMOs, and other company leaders often get caught up in the day-to-day work, so they have blinders on when it comes to their company's identity. They see the sales and the profit that great brands generate, yet they don't think their company is worthy of a brand. It's a shame to see, but that's what makes my work so rewarding. Our agency gets to open doors, show companies their possibilities, and uncover the heart of their brand. On a daily basis, we create compelling content that excavates the brand, outlines company beliefs, and resonates with consumers to differentiate them from the competition. This isn't a magic trick or a "glow-up" that fades at midnight; this is a rejuvenation and transformation of a company.

Change is scary, but empowering your challenger company through a brand is what will deliver exponential growth. At a certain size, companies become worried about maintaining what they've already built. It's not a one-or-the-other choice though; you can evolve your brand as you keep your clients, customers, employees, and stakeholders happy. Dare I say, even happier than before. Remember, it's not about uncovering something new but instead building your brand by highlighting the existing qualities of your company and amplifying its dreams.

I will say it again. Not only is branding accessible for challenger brands, but it is also a tool that is most powerful in the hands of challenger brands. Established brands know this and are now launching faux challenger brands within their large global portfolio of brands, or they simply buy them up. They know the special power of these brands to disrupt and become the next big thing. Hard to believe, right? Your category leader would rather be you on most days. As a challenger brand, you get to dream big and take this opportunity to create something larger than you may ever have imagined. A brand is your secret weapon against those established brands. Go for it. If you believe in it, then brand it and grow!

To conclude this chapter and incorporate all of my main points, I want to end with a small but important story of a brand that has personal meaning to me. Think of this as the moral we are left with at the end of most great children's stories.

The Woodcarver and His Wife. A Brand Fable.

I recently commissioned a job with a Maine woodcarver named Josh Landry, whose claim to fame at the time was completing an epic wood carving from a downed tree on the estate of Stephen King. I had two large old trees that had unfortunately come down, and I wanted to create something memorable out of those tree stumps that would make me smile each time I drove up the driveway to our home.

I found Josh on the internet and was immediately impressed with his craftsmanship. Due to a fortunate cancellation, he was able to take the job, and not only created a spectacular work of art for me but also became a good friend. As we were becoming acquainted with one another, one of the things I noticed was that his personal brand online didn't live up to the amazing talent that supported his family. I knew he was selling himself and his family short. As a favor to my newfound friend, I offered our agency's branding services gratis. While this humble man was making a fine living marketing himself as a wood carver, the image he had painted for himself was one of a local craftsman for hire by local villagers with limited financial means.

To take his brand to another level, we needed to expand the geography and financial means of his customer base. And to do that, we needed to elevate his brand story. If you go online to JoshLandry.com, you will see that, with a very small investment of our agency's time and talent, we were able to take all the compelling aspects of Josh's existing brand and simply re-cast them to support a new brand narrative. Josh was no longer a humble woodcarver for hire; he was a Chainsaw Sculptor to the Stars, entrusted with preserving the life stories of people and their families. Josh's new brand not only elevated his customer base but, more importantly, it elevated his commissions by setting him above and apart from other artisans. I restate my point—branding is a powerful tool at everyone's disposal.

Chapter three

7 Deadly Brand Fallacies

By now, you are probably starting to realize that I am a brand zealot and a huge advocate of "branding for all," but especially for challenger brands. And you'd be right.

I love building and watching brands transform any company, but watching the exponential effects it has on challenger brands is even more gratifying. I have seen it time and time again and this is what fuels my passion for marketing every day. So, if branding has such power to accelerate growth for challenger brands, why aren't more of them wielding their brands to slay goliaths rather than cowering in their shadows? In all of my years of shepherding brands, I have heard every reason for why a company feels it can't be a great brand. They typically come down to a predictable list of common fears and excuses.

Trust me when I say, the reasons that hold companies back from realizing their brand potential are grossly misplaced. The confusion and misinformation about what goes into building and maintaining a great brand have led to several consistent fallacies that put the brakes on valuable brand evolution for challenger businesses. In this chapter, we'll explore these common branding falsehoods and begin to debunk them.

The 7 Deadly Brand Fallacies

1) I don't have the budget to brand.

2) My customers don't care about branding.

3) Branding is a luxury.

4) I already have a brand.

5) Brands are too much work.

6) I don't have the vision to build a brand.

7) I don't know where to begin.

Branding Fallacy 1: "I Don't Have the Budget to Brand."

Of all the fallacies of brand building, this one may be the most commonly believed misconception.

The truth is, yes, you can spend millions creating your brand, and many companies do. But spending vast amounts of money on your brand doesn't make it inherently more successful. Companies of any size can brand, regardless of budget limitations. In fact, I have seen companies with some of the largest marketing budgets in the world simply end up clogging their brand message with the latest trends and tactics instead of using their brand as the lens through which they produce content. Conversely, I have seen smart, visionary companies with vastly smaller marketing budgets create brands that change the course of their company's future. How? You're sitting on the answer right now: your brand is found in your core values. You just have to take the time to mine them.

To find your brand, start with an exercise on brand excavation: dig deep into your company's history and ask yourself, what is at the heart of the business? Not the products, but the driving factors. You can do this step yourself (FOR FREE!) since this is a matter of analysis and reflection. And who knows your business better than you?

The cost of branding is not money; it's your commitment to finding and embracing the truths that are yours alone and that will inspire your employees and customers. In many ways, a new logo and tagline are more expensive in the long run than a true rebranding. They are visual trappings parading around and being held up as the sole expression of your brand; this can take your eyes off of the real work of articulating your one true brand. It's throwing money at the problem and hoping it resolves itself, whereas true branding will inform the entire approach. I tell every client: "The question isn't whether you can afford a brand; it's can you afford to not brand?" And that answer is a resounding NO! So, let's find a way to work within your budget.

You can, of course, hire a specialized branding agency like mine to guide you through the process, to do the work for you, or you can start the work yourself. There are benefits to finding a partner to work with when developing your brand. It will be an investment initially, but it may save you money in the long run by relieving you of the time investment and costly trial and error if you take it on yourself. And you will certainly appreciate the investment as your new brand ignites growth. But you can do this yourself! I guarantee that even a clumsily-worded brand promise, represented authentically as a reflection of the heart of your company, will take your brand further than if you never defined it at all. Don't let the fear of investment and costs stop you from finding your brand. Your passion and thinking are free. Let them go.

Branding Fallacy 2: "My Customers Don't Care About Branding."

To say your customers don't care about branding is like saying they don't care about relationships, connections, or love. They do care. Brand building is how companies evolve from having emotionless, short-term transactions to long-term relationships with their customers. But the reasons for starting your brand process today go even beyond the importance of your brand to your customer. Branding isn't just about your customers; it's about your employees, your product mix, your mission, and your experience. Branding is so much more than a catchy tagline to lure the next customer through your doors; it is a promise of how the world can expect you to act and engage with them. It puts a focus on people first and product second. Again, begin with the right questions and let your honest answers become the ingredients of your brand.

- What's your distinct value?
- How can you differentiate yourself from competitors?
- Do you have a defined purpose?
- What motivates your employees?
- How do you choose potential partners and acquisition?

You should be able to answer these without much thought. And what's more: your employees and customers should be able to answer them just as easily. Otherwise, your company and products are already on the path to becoming a commodity. There's too much competition vying for the attention of the same potential customers for you to win over *without* having a brand. You may still stubbornly think that you do not have to brand for your consumers, but you can bet that your competitors *will* brand, and without one, you'll be left out in the cold. Strive for better than existing for today; strive for putting your company on a clear visionary path with untold future potential. When you do, you will be on your way to embodying the traits that today's consumers are demanding of the brands they associate with. More on that in the next chapter.

Branding Fallacy 3: "Branding Is a Luxury."

When someone thinks of branding as a luxury, I believe it's because they don't fully understand what branding is. Keep in mind that metaphor of the piece of cake I shared in the introduction of this book. As long as you think of branding as the rich, colorful frosting that you slap on the top of your company, it will always seem to be a luxury you cannot afford. You have to think of your brand not as the icing but as the flour that you bake into every layer of your company. It is like the yeast that makes everything else rise. It's not a flurry of flashy advertisements, slick design updates, or a catchy new tagline—these are *expressions* of a brand but are not its entirety. These are the road signs that point to your brand. They each, in their own way, lead your customers to the emotional brand space that you have carefully carved out for yourself. If you approach them practically, brands can be used to improve all of your company's moving parts with very little downside and huge upside.

In fact, creating the pieces of a brand that only relate to marketing is the luxury: doing so offers short-term fixes that don't incorporate the vital brand steps necessary for sustainable growth. Companies can feel falsely confident as they check branding off their list until the next competitive onslaught forces the discussion once again. With strong budgets to drive heavy awareness and a formidable industry presence, larger companies have the privilege of relying on these short-term tactics to survive for just a bit longer than challenger companies could. But without strong brands, both sized companies will eventually be more at risk of succumbing to shifting market conditions.

Anyone out there can do what you do. Anyone can improve on your products and churn out new advertisements. But people can't copy your brand—it's at your core. Branding is the true necessity here, not a luxury.

Branding Fallacy 4: "I Already Have a Brand."

The general belief is that social media strategies count as branding; that the logo and tagline *are* the brand. While these assets are important, these tactics aren't the full representation of your brand on their own. They are creative signposts that lead to your brand.

Great brands should be a sustainable vehicle for a company's long-term vision; they are not quick, fuel-up television spots to spruce up your image. What I mean to say is that every action you take, whether it be a product development, logo change, advertisement, or an internal restructure, should be done so through the lens of your brand. A brand is not a uniform you can put on at the start of the work day and then remove at 5 pm. It should be embedded in every decision you make.

When a company asks me if I think it has a good brand, I often respond with: "If you aren't feeling your brand, you're failing your brand." What I mean is that great brands imbue life and meaning into companies. They are not tactics to be checked off. With the right brand behind you, your decisions are clear. Your mission is lived. If you can't say those things, then quite simply, you don't have a brand. Yet.

Branding Fallacy 5: "Brands Are Too Much Work."

I will be straight with you. Branding is a lot of work; there's no getting around the effort and care needed for it to succeed. Put good in, get good out. Put bad in . . .

There's a lot of early effort required to lay the groundwork, though it's made out to be much more difficult than it actually is. You have to look inward to be successful, starting with your team being on board with the branding journey.

The timeline of the initial branding stage varies and is mostly dependent on how fast clients want the process to move. However, we tend to follow the same chronology of process.

The first step is always the same: digging through company documents, mission statements, interviewing stakeholders, and much more in a creative exploration to define the brand. The amount of time spent in this excavation process depends on a client's budget and company size. Sometimes brand gold is lying in plain sight in a riverbed, and sometimes it's in the Mariana Trench at the bottom of the sea. But you don't know until you start looking.

At their core, businesses have a set of values, so finding the brand isn't usually the issue—the challenge is identifying the best language to express this core value. When we gather our analysis of the company's brand, it comes together in one pitch. The brand is conclusive, but how it's expressed is infinite and malleable depending how it is being used in your company.

From this point, it's a matter of looking at every aspect of your company through the lens of your new brand and articulating how these pieces will evolve. Establishing the framework for how your new brand will be implemented across your company requires deep thought but not a lot of time if you've correctly nailed down your brand. It's the rollout that takes time and careful planning. A brand doesn't emerge overnight, but, once the process is begun and your brand starts to emerge, you will be energized beyond belief and this will not feel like work to you. You will find yourself treading less water and excitedly creating more time to do this valuable work.

Branding Fallacy 6: "I Don't Have the Vision to Build a Brand."

Purge that bullsh*t. If you have the courage and intelligence necessary to own or run a company, you most definitely have the vision to unearth your brand. You set limits by doubting yourself and seeing your company as undeserving of a brand. There's no place for that mindset in the modern marketplace: you *deserve* a brand and more importantly, you *need* one.

The fallacies above are merely powered by doubt and other people's opinions. You didn't get to where you are by following Doubting Thomases, so reconnect with your purpose and go from there. It's incredible to see how previous clients have flourished once they've overcome these fallacies and see their brand uncovered. Many think it's unattainable until they see it shining in front of them—seeing is believing, after all.

When I walk clients through our exercises, I take them to the core of their businesses and show them the endless possibilities that come with engaging their brands. It is always rewarding to point a company down the right path and watch them take the reigns of brand development. Most are surprised at how everything they needed to build their brand was within them all along.

Branding Fallacy 7: "I Don't Know Where to Begin."

There's no blame game to play when it comes to understanding why brands are so misunderstood. Social media and the marketing industry are big culprits for confusing the process of true branding, but their existence is not the issue; the issue is that companies try to jump on new trends and become enamored with new technology at the expense of starting with the crucial first step: defining their brand.

By beginning with defining your brand, you will then know which technologies and online platforms you need to use to best nourish your brand. If you think of your brand as a book, there are a lot of different chapters and each of those chapters collectively tells your one true brand story. As the author of your brand, you wouldn't just jump into writing chapter six of your book without any idea of where it fits into the story. So why would you randomly choose a technology platform or ad campaign without knowing the role it plays in contributing to your overall brand story?

If you begin with the end in mind, the difficult decisions you need to make along your brand journey will soon begin to practically write themselves.

Moving Past The Brand Fallacies

A brand should be a guidebook that takes "lost" customers to the heart of your business. I always say that a brand is at its best when it mirrors the values and beliefs of your most passionate customers.

A lot of times you will find it's the numbers and data-obsessed people who feel reluctant about searching for their brand. Leaving behind the comforting reassurances of data for the uncomfortable work of brand building is a hard step. With my background as a creative professional *and* a businessman, I can speak both languages, that of CMOs and CFOs, as well as that of creative visionaries. I explain that creative brand building in itself is a business tool that can fit within and amplify a business plan. It's not some foreign practice that needs to be "managed" but rather a thoroughly proven business strategy that we're able to measure and utilize for growth.

A longer-term quantifier of your brand is looking at how your branding and marketing are evolving the conversations within your company, with your customers, and in your industry. Leaders can ask themselves:

- Is it challenging your efforts?
- Is it focusing on your initiatives?
- Is it amplifying customer conversations?

If you're not getting mostly "yes" to these questions, then you have to go back to the basics and reassess your defined brand or how you're delivering it.

As part of our agency's marketing approach, we do not leave branding results to chance. We hold weekly meetings with clients to discuss the analytics and effectiveness of our work together, and the overall health of the company. We don't propose a single band-aid solution to branding problems because we know that branding is more comprehensive than that. Anything less than a holistic brand vision won't deliver results.

Branding is where science meets art and only focusing on one part of that equation will not deliver the exponential results you expect. Move past all the reasons that are holding you back from being an admired brand and take baby steps if you need to. But never stop moving forward on discovering your brand.

Additional Resources

Some great resources for additional information include:

- *Find Your Why: A Practical Guide for Discovering Purpose for You and Your Team* by Simon Sinek

- *This is Marketing: You Can't Be Seen Until You Learn to See* by Seth Godin

- *Brand Thinking and Other Noble Pursuits* by Debbie Millman

Chapter four

Dare To Be Craveable

At our agency, Garrand Moehlenkamp, we hold brands in very high regard for the transformative power they have for our clients. To ensure that we are setting the right ambitions for ourselves and our clients, we have taken the extra step of not simply checking the branding box but creating a system that will ensure the creation of a specific kind of brand that will catapult your company. We call them Craveable Brands.

It's not some buzzword trend that will be replaced tomorrow—a Craveable Brand puts the customers' wants, needs, and desires at the core of everything an organization does in order to drive true connection.

We know that until we have built a brand for our clients that elicits a strong craving, (whether that craving be longing, lusting, drooling, or fawning—pick the craving of your choice) then that brand hasn't reached its craveable potential. This is the mission that drives every aspect of our agency.

> # Crave•a•ble\\
> ## Brand
> *a brand true to itself* that people don't just want, they **yearn** for — a brand that makes them feel more whole.

GROWING THE WORLD'S MOST

CRAVEABLE BRANDS

Craveable Branding is our agency's approach to uncovering more holistic customer insights that bring more empathy to our communications and elevate sales, loyalty and even advocacy.

We want your audience to do more than simply associate with your brand. We want them to feel they're made *whole* by associating with you. And during the times they're not engaging with your brand, we want them to feel like something is missing from their lives. Remember when you were younger and you would lose a tooth? That hole would feel absolutely huge when you stuck your tongue in it. *That's* the feeling we want. We want to have made your brand so connected to your customers' lives that when you aren't there, they *crave* to have you back.

It is an unfortunate truth that the default state of human existence is a relentless search to acquire the things that we feel will complete us. I would argue that we are all born complete and that all our problems arise when we fail to realize it, but that isn't the prevailing sentiment shared by most of the world. Insatiable longing for our missing half has always been a common theme in the plight of humanity, ever since Aristophanes told of how the Greek god, Zeus, fearing that a whole human would be more powerful than himself, split humanity in half creating man and woman and perpetual longing in the same stroke. Modern technology has only served to amplify our feelings of isolation by continually parading in front of all of us an endless stream of what appears to be much a happier and perfect population that doesn't actually exist. Sadly, the vast majority of us feel that we are incomplete beings and that there is always a void in us that needs filling, be that emotional or physical. And until that void is filled, we crave the ying to our missing yang like a fish craves water. By recognizing the profound effect these three cravings have on our lives and how they drive our actions including what we purchase, we can begin to have a more connected and empathetic approach to how we reach customers.

Our research shows us that those cravings typically fall into three basic buckets: our craving to satisfy our basic physical needs like food and shelter; our craving for social belonging; and our craving for personal aspiration. We crave nourishment when we are thirsty and hungry, but even more importantly, we crave validation, companionship, respect, intimacy, and friendship to nourish our sense of self. And while we can isolate these three core cravings into distinct buckets that drive all of our behaviors, rarely are a person's actions led purely by one of those cravings alone. In most cases, our behaviors are motivated by a combination of them simultaneously. Being able to understand and parse the complicated interplay of your audience's cravings at any given time will help you to create more meaningful connections. If you assume that customers are buying your product to satisfy an immediate physical need (but they are actually buying it because it evokes a strong emotional memory) you could be missing an opportunity to address what they're truly craving.

Meet
The Three
Core Cravings

By satisfying what people crave to feel whole, we can build deep-seeded connections.

Basic Need
How does this satisfy my basic, functional needs?

To gather deeper customer insights we started looking in a different place.

Social Belonging
How does this make me feel like I'm part of something bigger?

Personal Aspiration
How does this fulfill my craving to be my best self?

While all three cravings are always active, there are times when appealing to one craving over another is beneficial.

Each craving input can be leveraged singly or in combination at the right moment in the sales cycle.

Basic Need

Social Belonging

Personal Aspiration

Example: A craving related to basic needs may generate a visceral, short-term sale, while nourishing a customer's personal and social cravings will drive their loyalty and long-term connection with the brand.

In 1943, psychiatrist Abraham Maslow introduced a now famous hierarchy of humanity's needs. If you look at Maslow's Hierarchy of Needs, even back then, three out of the five levels of needs (love and belonging, esteem, and self-actualization) are emotional-based needs. Think about that. Maslow posed a radical theory that our physical survival as a species relied on being emotionally connected, but the foundation of his needs triangle consisted mainly of our physical need for safety and sustenance. After almost 60 years, his Hierarchy of Needs is still recognized as the preeminent accounting of what drives our actions daily. But times have altered what our most important needs are today.

With the advent of technology, the world has become more isolated from one another and our emotional need for personal connection and validation has become much harder to satisfy than our physical need for sustenance. As a result, Maslow's Hierarchy of Needs has become completely inverted as people place higher demands on their personal and social needs. Maslow himself foretold the scenario we are currently living in.

> It is quite true that man lives by bread alone — when there is no bread. *But what happens to man's desires when there is plenty of bread and when his belly is chronically filled?"*
> - Maslow

Our societal and individual needs have shifted

Once built to address basic needs, brands are helping people do more than just survive; they're helping them thrive.

Maslow's Hierarchy of Needs

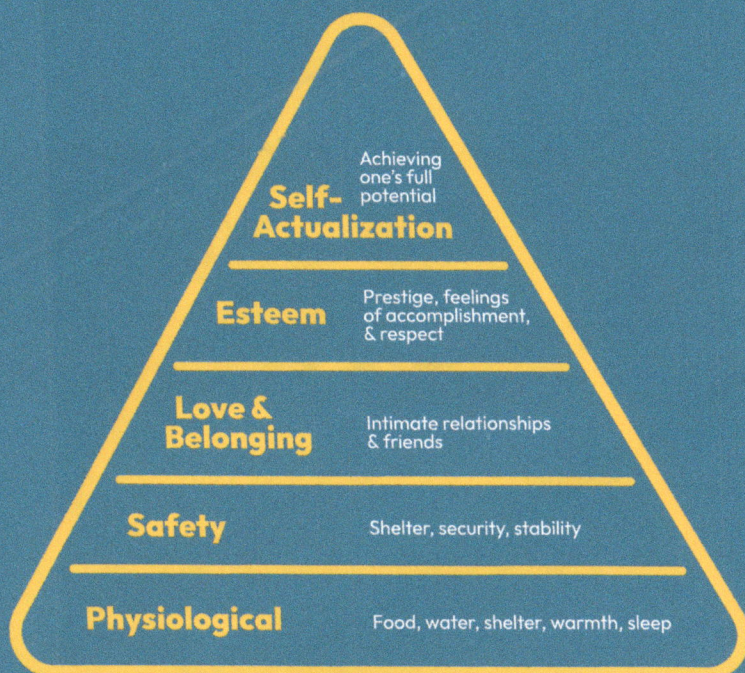

Self-Actualization — Achieving one's full potential

Esteem — Prestige, feelings of accomplishment, & respect

Love & Belonging — Intimate relationships & friends

Safety — Shelter, security, stability

Physiological — Food, water, shelter, warmth, sleep

Maslow's original hierarchy of needs in 1943 prioritized our physical needs over emotional.

Recognizing the deep emotional void that exists for so many, Craveable Brands are constructed to fill that void. They acknowledge that our individual and societal needs have shifted and that connection is the new currency. Companies can become white noise to consumers. It's only the brands with value beyond their products that reach today's customers in the way they want to be reached. Like no other time in the history of humanity, a myriad of modern factors has left millions of people around the world feeling isolated, with a steep increase in their cravings for connection. A recent article in the *New York Times* claimed that the world is in the midst of a "Loneliness Epidemic."[1]

> In small doses, **loneliness is like hunger or thirst**, a healthy signal that you are missing something and to **seek out what you need**. But prolonged over time, loneliness can be damaging not just to mental health, but also to physical health."
> — The New York Times

The world is starving for attention. And when we are starving, the search to remedy that situation becomes the dominant driver of our actions. But where can the world find connections at a time when we are becoming more and more isolated from one another?

We are seeing that the promise of a more connected world through technology has instead created the opposite. Yes, we can access millions of "friends" online with a keystroke, but we are quickly finding that those interactions are not truly satisfying our need for genuine connection. As a result, people's need for emotional kinship continues to grow. In response, people are getting much more creative with where they seek and find these emotionally kindred spirits. And one of those ways is through the brands they associate with. Brands have become metaphorical campfires where disparate groups gather around and find common ground, validation, companionship, and acceptance. Today's enlightened companies recognize the deeper unmet needs of these large groups of potential customers and are aligning their values and mission with them to create a bond that transcends a transaction. The evolution of this new customer/brand relationship, and the responsibility that comes with it, has inspired and shaped the way we think about our own brand purpose here at Garrand Moehlenkamp. And I hope that it begins to shape others in our industry as well.

WHY
CRAVEABLE BRANDS?

A manifesto of "why" we build Craveable Brands at our agency.

Because branding has become convoluted ...

Because people crave more than need ...

Because clients are overwhelmed ...

Because what you believe is bigger than what you sell ...

Because marketing typically talks down to people ...

Because marketing activates against a calendar ...

Because people crave connection ...

Because advertising is typically transactional ...

Because what you do is bigger than what you say ...

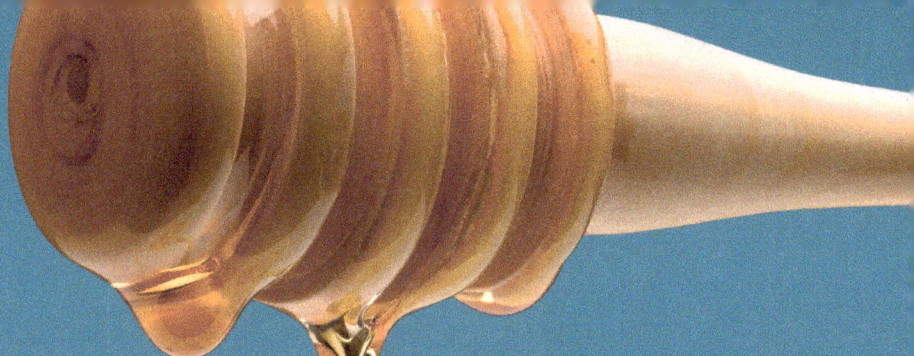

a Craveable Brand takes branding back.

a Craveable Brand flips Maslow on his head.

a Craveable Brand makes more sense of it all.

a Craveable Brand magnifies your brand truth.

a Craveable Brand builds them up.

a Craveable Brand activates a generation.

a Craveable Brand becomes their lightning rod.

a Craveable Brand transacts and transforms.

a Craveable Brand is a verb.

I will be the first to admit that coming from an "ad guy," this new age philosophical approach to branding may leave some skeptical. But in practice, it truly creates a mutually beneficial relationship with both the customer and company greatly benefiting on many levels. It will not only grow your company's bottom line, it will also grow your passion for your customer and why you go to work every day. When you put a brand out into the world that galvanizes your customers' views of themselves and their tribe, believe me, there is no better feeling. Why do fans of Harley Davidson willingly tattoo its logo onto their body, effectively becoming human billboards in the service of a motorcycle manufacturer? Because Harley Davidson has given them something in return that may be even more profound. It has given them an identity that clarifies their place on Earth. Yes, I stand by that statement. If I didn't believe that, I couldn't have spent so many happy years in this industry.

When you walk through the front doors of our agency, the first thing you'll see in big bold letters is a statement that says "Garrand Moehlenkamp. A Nourishing Agency." That is how we view the work we do. We never forget that on the other end of any branding communications we do for our clients is a customer that we seek to nourish on many levels. We need to leave them believing in something bigger than themselves, something they now see as worthy and special. Is that too lofty a goal for a branding agency? My partners and I don't believe so. And it shouldn't be for your company either. When you aspire for your company to develop a Craveable Brand, you will be developing a brand that connects with the world more deeply. It will receive a deeper level of brand loyalty in return. I did warn you earlier that I was a brand zealot, right?

It is not my intention in this chapter to sell you on my agency or our approach to branding. (You can call your branding approach whatever you like.) It is my intention to inspire more companies to stop putting out even more marketing noise into the world that insults everyone's intelligence and that nobody is paying attention to anyway. After decades of helping clients find their brand mojo, the Craveable Brand process is the most effective way I've found to drive financial growth for good companies and put positive life-affirming messages out into the world at the same time.

While many executives aren't in a position to go through the Craveable Brand process on their own and will need to seek help from outside agency partners, the basic principles of building a Craveable Brand are well within the comprehension of the average marketer professional, and I want to give you a good starting place here to begin your journey.

The first step to defining your Craveable Brand (or your branding process here) must be excavating your company's authentic vision and culture. The last thing any business wants is an ill-fitting outfit that isn't authentic to who they are and that is received by their audience as marketing puffery.

You can't force a fabricated version of your brand into the marketplace because savvy customers today will see right through it. To succeed, the brand you build must originate from the authentic core of your business through a brilliant melding of your rational, cultural, and emotional truths. We call them truths because they are true to what your company is, who it's for, and the conditions your business operates in. This is not the place for fancy flights of corporate fiction: these are the actual building blocks your authentic and timeless brand story will be built from, so be honest with yourself.

You can break these brand truths down into the three building blocks of your new Craveable Brand.

Rational Truths

Think of this as the "scientific" aspect of your brand. This should incorporate a precise breakdown of your business. What service or product do you provide? What is your day-to-day like? Who is your target audience and how are they evolving? What are your competitors doing? Where is your industry headed? These answers are all of the things that have made, and will make, your company a viable, rational choice for your customers. Here you must be a business visionary so that you express your brand in a way that will address and amplify all of your rational business realities and opportunities into the future.

Emotional Truths

Why does your business exist? What do you do for humanity? How do you connect with your audience? How does buying your product or service make their lives better? These are the kinds of questions you should be asking yourself as you think about your emotional truths. These are sometimes the hardest truths for rational, hard-driving pragmatists to excavate. So get a glass of wine and *feel* your brand. If you want your team and your customers to fall in love with your company, then you have to give them a brand to love. If they're not feeling your brand, you're failing your brand.

Cultural Truths

Your brand and your customers do not exist in a vacuum. At any given moment in time, their lives and attitudes are being shaped and reshaped by the existing conditions in the world they live in. These conditions influence how they think, act, and purchase. To not be aware of these conditions is to risk building brand castles in the sand. You want your brand to be able to ride out the inevitable waves of change, not be swept aside by it. This requires you to be aware of and evaluate your brand in the context of society and the world at large. How does your business fit into the bigger picture? Does it follow certain trends? What are the events affecting your customers' lives? Are they temporary or here to stay? Knowing the world you are launching your brand into will ensure its long-term survival and relevance.

Side Note: While it may be tempting to ride cultural trends opportunistically, you must avoid this! If your brand uniquely dovetails with current cultural conditions, ride them. If it doesn't, walk away and wait for the next cultural wave. The negative impact of your company being seen as disingenuous opportunist is far greater than whatever upside you had in mind.

Imagine these three levels of truths as overlapping circles in a Venn diagram, with your "brand" coming together at the center. In my experience, 90 percent of clients rely too much on the rational/scientific circle for marketing and neglect the strongly compelling opportunities that the other two bring to their brand story. Many people, especially those who are more comfortable with a rational approach, are often hesitant to engage in the creative and emotional process necessary to create their brand. What a miss.

The fact of the matter is that creativity and emotions are business tools, not frivolous concepts to be dismissed. People crave brands, not just from a physical and rational standpoint of what they bring, but perhaps more for what brands provide from an emotional standpoint as well. This is validated in Maslow's Hierarchy of Needs. But still, implementing these approaches is easier said than done for most business professionals. Oftentimes, you have to rely on your gut to find emotional connections with your potential customers. And rational business folk rarely trust their guts.

Let's take a look at an emotional and cultural brand success story of a company we work with named Biscoff. Those amazing little Biscoff cookies they serve on airplanes had a meteoric and somewhat unsuspecting rise to success. Not everyone knew its name, but people from all different backgrounds knew the signature cookies. When United Airlines pulled Biscoff from their flights, an enormous number of people wrote to them saying they were going to stop flying United if they got rid of those cookies. (Delta, United's competitor who was among the first to serve the same cookies, knew better than to bump Biscoff from their flights.) Why did travelers boycott? Did they think they were being ripped off? Did they fear going hungry? Have you seen how little those cookies are? No, the reason they threatened to boycott went well beyond the rational.

Biscoff had created a Craveable Brand that was bigger than a little cookie break. So craveable, in fact, that their customers were willing to go to the mat for them against United—one food editor going so far as to write an article entitled, "You Can Take My Leg Room, But You Can Never Have My Biscoffs."[2] Two days after it announced the discontinuation of Biscoff cookies, United Airlines did a 180 and announced that the cookies would return that spring.

To me, that's a revered place to be in. And Biscoff created that by distributing a massive amount of free samples—hundreds of millions a day! It created an indelible link between that little cookie and the adventure of travel. Biscoff approached our agency when it sought to transition that cult following into retail sales, a different kind of opportunity altogether. Biscoff already *had* the brand; because of that, it simply needed to capture the story of the amazing relationship between its cookies and flyers and translate it from 35,000 feet to ground level. With a strong brand, the way forward is much clearer.

Biscoff is a perfect example of the importance of emotional branding. Through the power of free samples and an on-point campaign, which tied the messaging to the freedom of air traveling. And it was able to translate these tiny airplane cookies into a cultural phenomenon.

This is precisely why you shouldn't limit your business exclusively to the realm of the rational. People find comfort in data, but they are moved by emotional and cultural factors. They desire more than a transaction from the companies they choose; they aspire to a relationship with a brand that sees the world the way they do. You won't be able to win over your customers as deeply without creating a cultural brand that evokes an emotional response. In response to the ever-increasing number of wayward brands I see out there, I adopted this three-pronged "truths" approach over my long career evolution from a young, award-hungry Chief Creative Officer to the more informed, thoughtful, and conscientious CEO that I hope I am today.

The long transition in my career from Creative Director to CEO was especially eye-opening. As a creative director, I was responsible for producing thousands of pieces of branding assets: campaigns, television spots, logos, digital assets, content, etc. I was elbow-deep in the creative execution of marketing materials and an advocate for "disruption" and creative excellence. But once I transitioned to CEO, I found myself further upstream in the process and closer to clients' true business needs. Instead of being solely responsible for producing "creative," I was responsible for something more demanding and tricky: the *ability* of the work we were producing to grow our clients' businesses and elevate their people and customers at the same time.

It was then that I started thinking as passionately about the problem as I did the creative solution—how could I help ensure that my agency was producing effective branding work that delivered tangible results? What were the replicable steps needed, and how could I guide my team and our clients to success? From those questions grew the three brand truths—rational, cultural, and emotional—that feed all of our insights and creation.

This strategy became even more useful when I branched out and started my own agency and I was presented with yet another new obstacle: how could I successfully brand my *own* branding agency? What was our own Craveable Brand? There are thousands of marketing and advertising agencies out there, so what was it that made our agency different? I needed to turn the same brand-building practices we deploy for our clients onto ourselves.

What I tell clients is fairly simple: we're not a marketing agency. We're a *nourishing* agency. Why nourishing? We knew that if we held every insight and solution to that high bar of nourishment, it would demand a much deeper and more evolved level of thinking on our part. Nourishing requires that you understand the opportunity and the audience at a high enough level to create something meaningful and additive to the audience. Very few products are so rare that all you need to sell them is awareness. We call ourselves a nourishing agency as a reminder that our solutions for clients need to be bigger than marketing and advertising; we need to create *true, enduring* brand connections that transcend the transaction.

If we all do our jobs right, your brand will actually nourish your customers, who will then nourish your brand in return. Yes, despite the bad rep marketing gets, I truly believe that brands can nourish the world with positive messaging. Our job is to help our clients give something back beyond a product. Simply put, their product is likely not that unique, therefore how can it effectively be the centerpiece of their branding campaign? The crux of any successful branding strategy is the quality, authenticity, and uniqueness of the story you're putting out there.

Let's look at the highly craveable Biscoff once again. The cookie itself is not particularly distinct; speculoos are quite common in parts of Europe, especially the Netherlands. And even in America, a shortbread cookie with ginger and nutmeg certainly doesn't stand alone in the grocery aisle. What separates Biscoff is more like a sensory memory than actual uniqueness, like getting buttery popcorn at the movie theater. Somehow popcorn and movies belong together in our minds, even though there are plenty of salty snacks you could have while watching a film. But the two have become linked in our minds, just like Biscoff and flying have. Brett Snyder, the president of the airline blog Cranky Flier, says of Biscoff: "We were on a flight to Hawaii when I was a kid, and my dad was like, 'I need more of these.' They gave him a whole bag. It's this treat when you fly, like ginger ale."[2] That's what a nourishing brand can give your business: it can create that connection in your customers' minds between your product and a feeling or an activity.

So, if Biscoff has a nourishing brand, what would the opposite of that look like? A transactional brand, perhaps? Tim Hortons is seen as *the* Canadian donut brand. In my opinion, it is probably as good of a company as Dunkin' when it comes to its people and products. However, even though it does have a small presence in the States, it's thought of as the Canadian Dunkin'; Tim Hortons never took on a brand persona that could compete with Dunkin' in the US. The business doesn't offer any positioning or alternative branding. It only offers an alternative product, and that's simply not enough to compete with a well-branded company. How could Tim Hortons expect to come in and win American hearts when "America Runs on Dunkin'"?

Tim Hortons may not be inclined to position themselves against America's favorite donut shop, but that doesn't mean others haven't. Here in Dunkin's own backyard, New England, Dunkin's toughest competitors are the Mom and Pop shops precisely because they've done the thing Tim Hortons hasn't: they've branded themselves *in opposition* to the big chain. Despite what you may think, local brands still have a strong presence and can carve a niche for themselves even in an oversaturated market where they are being outspent with marketing. How?

For one thing, consumers are much more concerned with ethical consumption than they used to be. Supporting local communities is a much bigger priority for the average shopper, so they are more willing to sacrifice convenience, consistency, and even cost for the sake of making sure the money they spend works its way back into the community. This gives small businesses an easy way to position themselves as competitors. On top of that, there's an emotional tug that comes with shopping locally; people are willing to spend a dollar or two more on their coffee if it means they get it in a cozy mug from their local shop. This is what I mean when I tell you that no matter how small your business is, it's big enough to brand. Passionately embrace your unique offering and tell that brand story from the heart and with conviction. Then you will have built a Craveable Brand.

Chapter five

The
Science
Behind
Emotional Branding

Perdue Chicken. For many of you, that's a brand you can reliably find in your grocery store, but it represents so much more for me. I grew up on a chicken farm—not just a few chickens squawking around the backyard mind you, but a full-fledged, chickens-to-the-rafters kind of chicken farm. One of the perks of being a grower for Perdue Chicken (at least my parents saw it as a perk) was that my family would sometimes get to attend their annual growers' convention in Salisbury, MD. Upon arrival at these conventions the "Perdue Parents" would herd all of their children into a single large conference/babysitting room while all of our parents would go off to sing, dance, and celebrate their collective allegiance to their fearless chicken leader, Frank Perdue.

In this chaotic childcare conference room, they graciously provided five toy trucks, a few dollhouses, some well-worn board games, as well as one large screen television that sat at one end of the conference room in front of a handful of chairs and bean bags and played a loop of all the Perdue Chicken commercials that aired that year. While most kids fought over the scant selection of second-hand toys, I would always settle down in front of that non-stop reel of Perdue commercials that were produced by the brilliant minds at the iconic Scali, McCabe, Sloves ad agency, one of the original bastions of MadMen. I found those commercials hysterical: "It takes a tough man to make a tender chicken," and the man in the commercial, Frank Perdue himself, looked just like a chicken to me. Amazing stuff for an impressionable young man!

Vintage Perdue Commercial that built an empire and inspired a young chicken farmer.

I was entertained for hours while my parents participated in the conference. My mother was fond of telling everyone that she would come back to pick all of her five children up, and I'd still be in the front row, laughing at the same commercials as if I was seeing them for the first time. (Were they that good or was I that easily entertained? Hmm, who's to know.) It's probably not a stretch to say that, deep down on a subconscious level, those early Perdue commercials heavily influenced my career choice to become an ad man myself. Over time, I developed this notion in my mind that commercials were their own brilliant art form and it began with those hilarious Perdue spots. So thank you, Frank and Scali, McCabe, Sloves.

I shared this story not to sidetrack down memory lane but because I often wondered why I connected with those commercials to the point where I was willing to sit still for so long when most times my mother couldn't get me to sit for five minutes. What was going on in my little head all those years ago that would cause me to spend not just a couple of hours but the rest of my life obsessed with every frame that builds a 30-second commercial?

As it turns out, my being drawn to those humorous Perdue commercials wasn't as strange or uncommon as it may seem. In fact, it was science. That's right, there is good old data-backed science that validates how our actions are overwhelmingly driven by emotions. I can't possibly go into all the available research on the subject here in these pages, but I highly recommend that anyone in marketing or sales read a couple of the books that go deeper into the subject (some of my favorites can be found at the end of the chapter). The net takeaway is that when it comes to making a lasting impression, emotions matter most. That is why the memory of those Perdue commercials is as vivid to me today as the day I sat mesmerized in front of that screen watching the exploits of Frank Perdue play out.

That original emotional impression I had in the Perdue conference room as a boy is the kind of lasting emotional impression that, to this day, I encourage my clients to demand from their brand. Our agency approaches our clients and their customers as thinking, feeling human beings who are keenly aware and discerning of the companies they're engaging with. The emotional power of the content you produce matters, particularly if you're striving to create something that truly resonates with your audience.

Connection is the New Currency — and brands are key purveyors

People don't rally around a product, they rally around each other. And, the expectation of brands in building these connections is high.

High expectations: what today's consumers want from brands

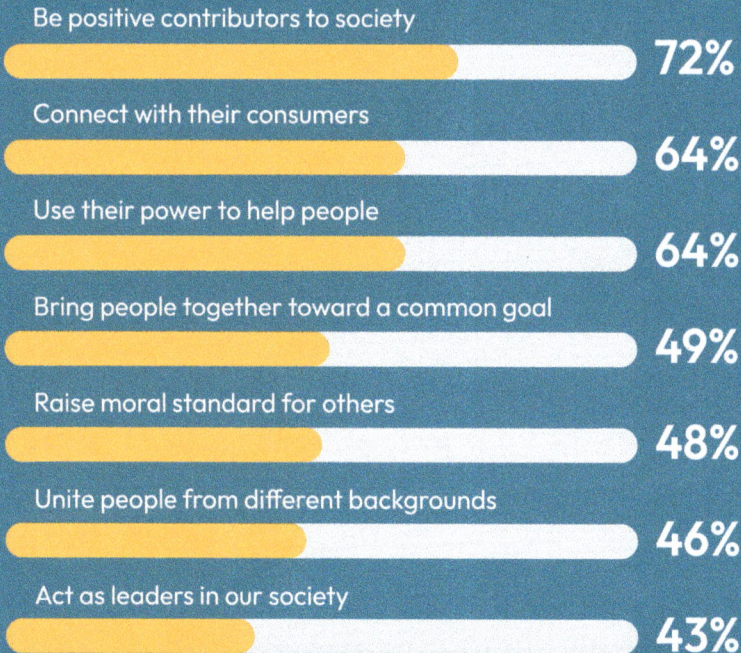

Be positive contributors to society
72%

Connect with their consumers
64%

Use their power to help people
64%

Bring people together toward a common goal
49%

Raise moral standard for others
48%

Unite people from different backgrounds
46%

Act as leaders in our society
43%

https://sproutsocial.com/insights/data/social-media-connection/

At our agency, we represent many food and beverage clients, whether they be large restaurant franchises, consumer packaged goods, or beverage brands. As you may already know, there is no category that is more emotionally charged for all of us than food. That is because most of us were brought up to believe that food is love.

Mothers, from time immemorial, have demonstrated their love for their children by serving up heaping plates of carbo-loaded bear hugs. Most people do not process their food choices rationally. If they did, this country would be a lot healthier, as this story will attest.

I recall sitting at a meeting with the CEO of one of our largest restaurant clients many years ago having a very serious discussion about some drastic menu changes they were considering implementing. The client was considering completely overhauling the chains' entire menu to address a *New York Times* article that had run recently—the article had put large food chains in the hot seat to offer healthier choices for consumers.

This CEO was convinced the bottom was going to fall out of his business unless he swapped out his tried-and-true menu favorites for a bevy of healthier options. Serendipitously, the day before coming to this meeting, I had read an article in Restaurant News featuring the then-CEO of Carl's Jr. The interview covered the outcry from national media outlets for an increase in "better for you" dining options. In response, the Carl's Jr. CEO shared a very interesting story. He explained that every time he added another audaciously delicious, aka fattening, ingredient to his burgers, Jay Leno would go on the late show and talk about the audacity of Carl's Jr. to add two eggs to a burger! Did it scare away customers? Far from it.

Every time Jay decried the new ingredients, particularly from a health perspective, customers lined up at the doors the very next day to be the first to try the new mouth-watering creation. Their CEO said it had become his strategy to continually find the next ingredient that would compel Jay to talk about it on air and drive sales. So, while the national media was hyping the story of a national backlash towards healthier options, the public was behaving in a very different way. While Carl's Jr.'s customers understood the rational reasons for a healthier lifestyle, it wasn't a reflection of their behavior. Some would say they were acting irrationally. But in actuality, they were behaving in the way they had always behaved, emotionally.

This "irrational" behavior defies rational thought. But that is the thing that companies must understand if they are to connect with their customers. One of the key benefits we have identified for building a Craveable Brand is that it builds irrational loyalty. People sometimes cannot even tell you *why* they are so committed to certain brands because their loyalty is driven by deeply ingrained emotions that they themselves aren't always aware of. But if you can understand these emotional drivers and then appeal to them, it gives your company a distinct advantage over your competitors.

In sharing Carl's Jr. story with our client, we were able to keep him from overreacting to the news article and instead implement "better for you" menu changes without abandoning the iconic dishes that their customers came for. Bullet dodged.

In our initial presentations to clients, we will always find a way, whether it be with a brand video, a montage board, customer testimonials, or a long-form manifesto to bring together all of their core values and their vision and bring to life the kind of emotional connection that we would seek to elicit with their customers. I believe it is vitally important for our clients to experience firsthand the kind of emotional impact their brand can have on their customers before we can expect them to get fully behind it. If we can't get them emotionally behind our proposed direction first, then we've failed them as their brand creator and storyteller.

You can tell when something has the potential to be deeper, to fully connect viewers, when it pulls on something more than rational. This reaction is based on brand psychiatry. Addressing consumer needs and invoking a sense of nostalgia can tap into a consumer's emotional core. Perdue chicken is nostalgic for me because of the strong memories I associate with it. The autobiographical memory, which tracks episodes of our lives, is triggered when we are reminded of these past moments. We then re-experience the emotions felt during those episodes.[1] That means if I'm at a store torn between Perdue and Simply Organic chicken, I'm likely to choose the former because of the nostalgia their memorable ads evoked in me. That emotion may even be powerful enough to influence me to cook chicken instead of beef, simply because of the enduring connection I have with Perdue.

Forbes calls emotions "the super weapon of marketing and advertising." Just as there are three primary colors (red, yellow, blue), people have four basic emotions: happiness, sadness, fear/surprise, and disgust/anger.[2] This ties into Maslow's Hierarchy of Needs. When you create and articulate your brand, you need to speak to the fears, wants, and needs of your audience if you want your message to resonate. These emotions drive our basic needs and all decision-making: Will that sweater keep you warm (reduce fear of cold)? Is buying that new phone going to make you happy?

Since we live in a culture of immediacy, brands have to be prepared to create a connection and capture the attention of consumers *without* relying on making the features seem frivolously catchy. Emotion needs to be the crux of your brand, not the technical jargon of what differentiates you. *Psychology Today* reported that "Functional magnetic resonance imaging (fMRI) shows that when evaluating brands, consumers primarily use emotions (personal feelings and experiences), rather than information (brand attributes, features, and facts)."[3] This emotional response will influence their decision-making when it becomes a choice between two brands.

Consider an everyday product that many people purchase: milk. Do you buy the brand you enjoyed as a child? Do you select the generic brand? Or do you seek out the hormone and antibiotic-free option? No matter which you choose, whether you're aware of it or not, it's likely an emotional decision—the nostalgic draw of carefree childhood days or the desire to be healthy by consuming from a healthy source (the cows).

The cows behind the milk have always been the focus of Hood® dairy farms, though not many consumers saw it. In creating marketing with Hood® over the past three decades, our agency always appreciated the emphasis executives placed on having happy, healthy cows to produce better-tasting and healthier milk. Everyone likes to see animals, it is just a marketing fact—Geico continually plays that card brilliantly. By creating a transparent relationship between the source of the milk (the farmers and the cows themselves) to the consumer, the entire dynamic became emotionally charged. And with that small change to align the marketing materials with the brand, Hood® dairy products rose to the top of family shopping lists.

Whether it's through our work with Hood® or any of the hundreds of other clients we've had the pleasure of partnering with, we know that the key to customer relationships that stand the test of time is creating emotional connections. At Garrand Moehlenkamp, we call ourselves a nourishing agency because it reminds us that we're there to create something more with our clients than a fleeting, one-ditch effort. It compels us to come together with our clients as a team and ask:

- Is your brand providing more than just a transaction to your customer?
  - *If yes, is this notion articulated in their brand and conveyed in their content across all aspects of their company?*
- Is your brand bigger than the products or services you're selling?

- Only the great brands that truly incorporate their brand at all levels of the company can say yes to this.
- Is your brand uniquely authentic to you and your values?
  - And maybe most importantly, do you *feel* your brand?

Sometimes I give myself goosebumps when I'm presenting to a company's owners. We take their mission statement and values, and we translate them into a beautiful brand. I've seen hard-boiled executives shed actual tears in meetings when seeing their brand truly realized for the first time. It wasn't because my presentation was that good, rather, it was that the presentation emotionally brought to life what they had always felt deep down about their company but had never seen articulated. The emotional response these owners show when first meeting their brand is the same reaction we strive to create in their consumers.

While the benefits of emotional branding are countless, there are third rails that you must stay away from. In inviting your customers into an emotional connection, you are asking for more than a transaction. You are asking them to open up and engage with your company on a deeper and more personal level. That type of connection comes with more responsibility. If you ask your customers to embrace their authentic selves and find common ground with your company, you better be sure that you are demanding the same authentic representation of yourself. If you greet your customers with an inauthentic brand, it will have the absolute reverse effect on what you're trying to do. In asking your customers to enter into an emotional bond with your company, you are asking for something more personal than just a clinical transaction. And when a customer finally chooses to enter that type of relationship with your company, they will expect more of you in return. They will hold you to a higher standard. If you undermine that relationship by being bad actors, they will feel betrayed and will let the world know.

We see our clients' customers as thinking, feeling human beings who are keenly aware of the companies they are choosing to bring into their life. So, it's not just about the speed of how quickly you can capture their attention, but how you can earnestly capture their hearts and minds. That level of authenticity is determined by an organization's commitment to its own brand and its continuous efforts to nourish that brand. Never underestimate the average consumer's ability to sniff out inauthentic bullsh*t. Learning to maintain sanity in a world full of noisy, screaming ads has left consumers with a highly trained radar to filter out all but the most relevant messages to them.

At the end of the day, it's easy to forget facts and product features, but as humans, we are programmed to remember and retain the emotions we experience at a far higher rate. When a brand incorporates emotional messaging, it forges a more effective and "sticky" approach: the start of a Craveable Brand.

Additional Resources

Maslow's Hierarchy of Needs is one example we discussed in the chapter, but there are a lot of great books and articles that explore the science of how emotions drive our everyday decisions. Some of my favorites include:

- *Emotional Branding: The New Paradigm for Connecting Brands to People* by Mark Gobe
- *How Emotions are Made: The Secret Life of the Brain* by Lisa Feldman Barret
- *Descartes' Error: Emotion, Reason, and the Human Brain* by Antonio Damasio

Chapter six

Craveable
Brands
Endure

Sometimes, in understanding how to navigate the future, we can simply look to the past. I think that can certainly be said of branding. Branding has evolved since its early days. In the past (let's say pre-1960), a company's "brand" was organically defined by its products, services, and window dressings, such as its design and packaging. Any brand those companies developed in the minds of their customers was, in a sense, accidental and subjective depending on the viewers' particular biases and the company's ad spending.

Sure, many of those companies would articulate their values and wanted their employees to know them, but there wasn't quite today's proactive commitment to curating their brand and infusing those brand values into marketing efforts and every other aspect of their company. Our definition of brand today is much more highly evolved and strategic than that of the past.

Companies of bygone decades solely relied on advertisements to raise awareness of their products, not to establish company values that would resonate with their customers' own values, as a brand is meant to do. Looking back, history has proven that the brands that have thrived and endured are the ones that understood the power of establishing an emotionally compelling brand and nourished it through the years. Even as the world changed dramatically around them, they steadfastly held onto the vision and beliefs at the core of their brands. Even then, these brands knew that if they based their brands on timeless values that we have all embraced since the beginning of time, they themselves just might turn out to be timeless as well.

Now, it may seem like a no-brainer that massive companies like Coca-Cola, IBM, and Ford are enduring brands. But are they Craveable Brands?

Here, I would like to present an opinion that runs counter to all the "Top 100 Brands" lists out there. I believe that years ago, companies with a combination of a great product, strong leadership, and fortuitous market timing could stand the test of time. But I believe that what we have here is a chicken and egg question. Did those companies endure because they adopted a compelling brand philosophy from the beginning, or have they become renowned brands because they were exceptionally well-run companies that have stood the test of time?

I would argue that the latter is true. Many of the companies that sit atop those "Top 100 Brand" lists published each year would be more appropriately classified as iconic companies vs. brands. And you could argue, why does it matter? It doesn't—to the casual observer. But to anyone sitting at the helm of a company with the responsibility of assuring its long-term success, it matters. A lot.

As we mentioned earlier in the book, the old rules for building a successful company have changed dramatically. We live in a time where true product innovation is rare, and customers are compelled by the way your company acts more so than what you sell. So looking to enduring brands of the past for answers to the way forward could be misleading. However, there are those companies in the "Top 100" lists that did have the foresight from their very beginnings to build their company on a foundation of brand values that have grown and sustained them for decades. The difference is that some were built as Craveable Brands while the others have simply become Iconic Brands. To me, the other reason for recognizing the difference is that, while hard work and superior business savvy will always remain integral to a company's growth, today's market environment is much too complicated to solely rely on those virtues as the engine of your success. You need a magic sauce that no one else can duplicate because it is inextricably tied to the very heart of what your company is—and that magic sauce is your brand.

The simple principles required to create an enduring Craveable Brand are accessible to everyone, regardless of budget. You can create exponential growth on the back of a Craveable Brand beginning today and far into the future without the need to continually feed the marketing and PR beast to maintain your iconic status. Because your company chose to align your values to those of your customers, those customers become lifelong ambassadors. In representing what your audience craves most in the world, your company becomes the living embodiment of the sustenance they seek both physically and emotionally. And what is it that people crave most? Come with me as we explore some prominent brands that have stood the test of time. You may start to see how those three timeless core cravings (basic needs, social belonging, and personal aspiration) drove customer loyalty then as strongly as they do today. These are the brands that leveraged them to endure.

Ben & Jerry's

Electric Egg Ltd. stock.adobe.com

Much like Dunkin', Ben & Jerry's is another New England business that's flourished beyond the region to become a national success. Founded in 1978 in Burlington, Vermont, the company went from a single ice cream parlor to a multinational brand over the course of a few decades. It's more than a range of flavored ice creams. Its mission centers around three key elements: a product mission, an economic mission, and a social mission (very closely aligned to basic core cravings).[1]

The product mission of "euphoric concoctions" promises customers quality. Sure, all businesses offer some degree of guaranteed satisfaction but not all take on the commitment to top-level, environmentally-conscious ingredients. It excludes GMO ingredients and produces vegan and dairy-free ice cream alternatives for its relevant customer base.

The economic mission is a commitment to stakeholders and employees alike, with an emphasis on creating sustainable financial growth in conjunction with expanding opportunities. Businesses are for-profit by nature, but the Ben & Jerry mission follows a purpose-driven avenue that uses the profit to produce greater value. *That* is unique.

Ben & Jerry's may have embraced elaborate flavors with memorable names, but its commitment to social causes has led the brand to endure. It has joined all the conversations: environmental issues, criminal justice reform, refugee rights, LGBTQ+ rights, climate justice, etc. And it works because it's authentic to the brand rather than a pandering corporate move to increase profits. Some moves—such as the decision to not sell Ben & Jerry's in Occupied Palestine Territory in response to Israel's violation of Palestinian rights—have brought considerable criticism.[2] However, the proud Jewish founders, Bennett Cohen and Jerry Greenfield, recognized the importance of their voices in the conversation. Anything else would be inauthentic and "inconsistent with our values." This takes brand values to the ultimate level, leaving no surprise that the brand has endured.

From an article by Jay Curley, Global Head of Integrated Marketing at Ben & Jerry's, the brands that last are purpose-driven brands that "use [its] brand voice to advance [its] values and be an advocate for real social change in the world . . . it means you sell not just more stuff but big ideas."[3]

Based on Ben & Jerry's continued success as the leading ice cream brand of 2022 (with sales of approximately $282 million), it's clear that this 6P approach—Purpose, Policy, People, Power, Publishing, and Pop Culture—resonates with customers in a way that makes it a Craveable Brand.[4]

Apple

Think Different. It's subtle, easily dismissed as a mere tagline until you dig deeper to realize that those two words embody the creativity and passion that has inspired a revolutionary tech company and its rabidly loyal customer base for close to four decades. But a simple catchphrase didn't lead to the $394.3 billion in revenue that it achieved in 2022. The promise had to move beyond the page in order to endure. Apple uses the emotion behind the purchase, humanizing the brand by selling ideologies in conjunction with its products.[5]

It's not *just* a computer: it's the way you are creatively empowered to move from your side hustle design work to a full-blown startup. They aren't just earbuds: they're wireless earbuds that give you the freedom to be inspired by your own personal soundtrack as you move from the gym to your job. The Apple promise goes well beyond the promise of better technology to igniting potential and creativity and because of that commitment, it endures.

It's practically a cult following by now. People don't simply switch over to Microsoft or Samsung products after years with Apple. Sure, some of that can be attributed to preferring the known of Apple to learning a new system, but it wouldn't account for the millions of people who trumpet Apple's superiority. Much of its success is attributed to its user-friendly products and emphasis on the user experience. How do you establish a fan base? Launch quality products. How do you *maintain* a fan base? Listen to their needs and adapt to the changing times. That's Apple in a nutshell. From the clunky original desktop to the sleek iPhones and iPads, the products and accompanying gadgets have allowed consumers to "think differently" and achieve new heights in business and leisure pursuits.

LEGO®

In 2015, LEGO® overtook Ferrari to become the world's most powerful brand. In that same year, the profits quadrupled, actually outperforming Apple.[6] (In fact, LEGO® has been called the Apple of Toys.) A remarkable feat by any standard, but made even more so by the fact that LEGO® is a toy company that has been around for almost a century selling essentially the same block system all those years.

Many people are shocked to hear just how long LEGO® has been pumping out bricks. Since 1932, LEGO® is a company that has managed to stay eternally youthful in the eyes of the world and its dedicated customers who range in age from eight to eighty. And it has done so by staying true to its brand vision, which the LEGO® Corporation states is "to inspire and develop the builders of tomorrow. The Kirk Kristiansen family aims to fulfill the mission of helping all children grow and develop to their full potential through creative play." Their ultimate purpose is to inspire and develop children to think creatively, reason systematically, and release their potential to shape their own future—experiencing endless human possibility.[7]

Wow! No doubt there are business strategies that accompany those inspiring words, but that is not what has driven this company to the pinnacle of business success. To be clear, LEGO® has had to survive dark periods of business headwinds.

From its founding in 1932 until 1998, LEGO® has never posted a loss. In 2003, it suffered a reversal of fortune. Sales were down 30 percent year-on-year and it was $800 million in debt. Then CEO Jorgen Vig Knudstorp was famously quoted as saying, "We are on a burning platform ... [and] likely won't survive."[8]

But by abandoning a wayward diversification strategy into clothing and theme parks, LEGO® turned the situation around by doubling down on its commitment to its founding brand principles.

LEGO® found what all enduring brands discover; by fiercely embracing your brand principles, a company can evolve to ride the ever-shifting currents of the marketplace. Through the years, LEGO® has brilliantly partnered with Hollywood to create new LEGO® properties. It created new product lines that have brought girls into the LEGO® phenomenon. Found new ways for aging LEGO® fans to continue to be fans with LEGO® Robots for teens and LEGO® Architecture Kits for Adults. And most recently, it is bridging the world between the physical and the virtual with LEGO® Life. All of this change is anchored in its same powerful brand mission to inspire and develop the builders of tomorrow. A brand that has inspired the creation of over four billion mini-figures. Now that is a return on brand.

Disney

I feel the need to caveat this next enduring brand example in the same way that news broadcasters will let you know when they are about to deliver a story on a company that is paying their salaries.

I have been a diehard Disney fan ever since my first magical encounter with them as a child. Since that first visit to Disney World, I have been a member of their Disney Vacation Club for almost 15 years, with another 35 years remaining on my membership. And I'm thinking of extending my membership! Sick. I know. And it's a very hard notion for my creative network to wrap their heads around. After all, us creative types are supposed to support our image as a jaded and brooding slice of humanity. Disney is all light and sunshine. What gives? Sorry, my skeptical brethren, I absolutely LOVE this last, little bastion of hope and optimism that Walt began creating almost 100 years ago. Manufactured or not, I choose to be a doe-eyed believer in the whole Disney brand experience. And I am not alone. Today, Disney's parks around the world will see 62 million visitors a year.

All those years ago, Walt Disney tapped into something very pure and emotional as he poured his talents into creating the world's first animated movies that brought the unimaginable to life. I believe he knew from the very beginning that the world would always crave a little magic in their lives that would transport them to their happy place. A place that, for most of us, is inextricably linked to our childhood. To be able to be transported back to a time of innocence and complete trust in the world is a craving that drives all of us, whether we acknowledge it or not.

And with every movie, short film, stuffed animal, TV series, and book, Walt Disney creates a portal to that cherished place. Is it intentional? Yes. Does it make the experience any less amazing? Only if you harden your heart to it (sadly, some people's happy place is a dark place). Either way, Walt and his ensuing empire have become vicious defenders of the Disney brand. It spills out of every corner of its parks and from every frame of its movies. And I for one never tire of hearing "Have a Magical Day" after every encounter with its cast members. While I know that I may have exposed myself as a raving fan these last few pages, that is the point. Companies like Disney that build themselves around an unwavering emotional connection to their customers create a bond that goes way beyond a transaction to what we call irrational loyalty. If Disney can crack the crusty outer shell of a hardened, cynical ad guy like myself, what chance does an ordinary civilian have against its brand of magic?

As change is being thrust upon the world at an unimaginable pace, and technology quickly replaces authentic human connection with online posting, those magic moments that transport us to a more innocent place will only become more and more highly craveable. And as long as the Disney brand continues to stand as protector and purveyor of that innocence, it will endure.

Habitat for Humanity

You have heard me and other brand believers say it before, "It's not what you do, it's why you do it that matters to the world."

Sometimes a company's "why" is so pure and compelling that it defines and communicates every aspect of your brand with very little need for marketing.

Habitat for Humanity's roots began in Millard and Linda Fuller's attempt to develop the concept of "partnership housing." Those in need of housing would work side by side with volunteers to build affordable housing at no profit.[9] The new homeowners' house payments were combined with fundraising and no-interest loans to create "The Fund for Humanity" to continue building homes for those who need them. In 1976, the Fullers founded Habitat for Humanity International, and it has continued to serve communities to this day. Products are often trying to find their purpose, the heart of their brand, but this isn't necessary for Habitat. Their work speaks for itself.

What I find most interesting about Habitat for Humanity is you don't see many advertisements for them. The brand is solidified and communicated in ways outside of traditional marketing, like its actions, PR, word of mouth, etc. This doesn't mean that its presence is stronger or weaker than other organizations, or that it doesn't participate in marketing tactics at all, but it shows the diversity in what it means to build a brand. Habitat for Humanity's brand truth is quite apparent: everyone deserves to be a part of a home and a community. A community building homes for each other tells the Habitat for Humanity story better than any ad campaign. Its mission *is* its brand since everything Habitat for Humanity does continues to nourish what it is as an organization and the work speaks for itself.

Who your brand attracts and who you choose to partner with are incredibly important for building an enduring brand. When you picture those involved with Habitat for Humanity, it's often a unified image: volunteers framing a house, all wearing the same blue branded shirts and hard hats, working together. The brand's audience speaks for itself in an overwhelmingly positive way, especially when you see a volunteer like former President Jimmy Carter. Since 1984, Carter and his wife promoted the work of Habitat for Humanity by actively participating in it, working alongside over 103,000 volunteers in 14 countries to build and repair 4,331 homes.[10] Habitat consistently works with celebrities to raise awareness, accessing various groups of fans: Garth Brooks, the Scott Brothers, David Letterman, etc.[11] By tapping into these key partnerships, Habitat for Humanity builds its brand awareness and further legitimizes itself.

In essence, Habitat for Humanity is able to match its message with its capabilities. Its commitment to communities is more than just building as many homes as possible; advocacy efforts, policy reform, financial education, and disaster response provide sustainable brand nourishment that grows with the organization. By staying true to these brand values, it is able to partner with businesses and figureheads who want to be a part of that brand; those partners' participation in the brand strengthens it even further, and now it has created a brand loop that continually nourishes itself.

Look to Endure

Looking back on all of these examples, the easiest step to creating a Craveable Brand that can truly endure is a commitment to your "why" and not your "what." By defining what your brand stands for, watching where the world is going, and imagining your brand living out into the future, you discover the ideals worth committing to. This is no easy task, and it requires a lot of research, but the rewards are priceless.

It is far easier today to understand what makes a great brand because of the courage that past companies adopted, like the ones featured above, in order to build their companies on something bigger than hard work and hope. Through their enduring success, today we are able to see the extreme value in placing your company's future on something that we all may have thought frivolous until we gazed upon their greatness. Today more companies than not are following suit. Companies such as Yeti, lululemon, LaCroix, JetBlue, and countless others have learned from the past and are setting the new standard for how to build an emotional brand that endures into the future.

Chapter **seven**

SO YOU THINK
YOU
HAVE A
BRAND!

I've spent a lot of time talking about the power of branding, crafting your vision, embracing the heart of your business, and brands that have succeeded in doing all of the above. Before we talk further about ways of creating your own Craveable Brand, I think it is also important that we discuss what a brand is *not*.

In the brilliantly poignant words of country music singer Kenny Chesney: "We still don't know what love is, but we sure know what it's not."[1] Finding your brand is a big, emotional process into the unknown, and it's often not easy to put your finger on what it is until you have it. But you will know when you find your brand because you will feel it in your bones. Don't get me wrong, there are reliable steps to guide you to your true brand, steps that we discuss in this book, but for much of the process, you are feeling your way to it. You may recognize this concept: just as customers need to feel your brand and resonate with it, so must you.

Everyone's brand journey is personal to their company and who they are, so it goes without saying that your path will be unique. If brand-building was a cookie-cutter process, it would produce cookie-cutter results. That doesn't mean I'll leave you to flounder through the brand-building journey alone; there are helpful signposts to let you know which directions to *not* take on your way to finding your brand. And recognizing those signs is crucial.

It may sound strange to dedicate a whole chapter to the antithesis of a brand. Why wouldn't I just use this space to further explain the idea of a brand and crafting your own? I think it's important because I've seen far too many of my past clients who had stopped searching for their true brand because they thought they had already found it. Or to be more precise, they had been convinced by "experts" that they'd already found a brand when what they actually had was just a few disparate elements of a brand. Road signs pointing hither and yon.

In reality, far too many times all they actually have is a fake Rolex sold to them by an opportunistic ad agency on a NYC street corner. While this sounds like a jab at my own industry, it isn't too far from the truth. We know not to look for an authentic Rolex in the street, but if you didn't speak the language or know the culture, you would likely be sold on the promise of that fake Rolex. And so it is with the marketing industry: they sell clients on an incomplete model of what their brand is. Just like a fake Rolex, this brand is only a fraction of the quality. The collapse of great branding is an industry-wide failure, and our industry only has itself to blame.

To say the marketing industry has gone through a quantum shift in the last two decades is a gross understatement. Just look at the rise in the number of companies that list themselves as full-service marketing agencies. Now add to it the number of companies selling "fresh" marketing tools and technology. Big promises without the structure in place to follow through on them.

I've been in this industry for over 30 years, and I can't even keep up with every new "must-have tool" that agencies are selling. What makes it even more confusing is that on top of the surge of technology and endless trends, almost every one of these new agencies with a tool claims to be a one-stop shop with all of the answers for your company. Including branding.

You can get over 6000 full-service marketing agencies all pushing to speak with you about these tools you "can't live without."[2] Most often, these "full-service" agencies are actually specialists in building out just *one* aspect of your brand. And they may actually deliver that one part *really* well, but it won't give you the complete, sustainable brand you're looking for to ignite your entire company.

I don't mean to insinuate that marketing agencies are being deceptive. While it's cliche to portray our industry as packed with slick salespeople, I believe the more likely truth is that the agencies themselves have just never had the experience of crafting a truly great brand. Without that experience and context, they are defining a brand in a very diminished way that suits their purposes. They've confused the tools to assist in building your brand with the brand itself.

Without first-hand experience, people only see the problem through the narrow lens of their specialty. It's like the old saying "When you're a hammer, everything is a nail."

I have immense empathy for CMOs today trying to sort through all of the tactics, techniques, and agencies to build and differentiate their brand. Choosing the wrong agency can take you down a primrose path and divert your best brand-building efforts for years. And your time of inaction is time that could have been spent getting a supercharged brand built right out of the gate. Sadly, it won't be until the next CMO comes in to replace you that you realize you were duped. This chapter will explore what a brand is *not,* so you don't become the CEO or CMO who wastes years in brand purgatory until awoken by that dreaded call from the board.

Asking the Tough Questions

So if you suspect that you may be sitting on a faux brand, how do you know for sure?

I don't want to be the bearer of bad news, but if my perspective will get you back on the road to building your true brand, then you can happily shoot the messenger. First, let's start with some very simple signs that may point to the possibility that your current "brand" may be just a shell of the brand you were meant to be.

- If you can't connect your brand to your core values . . .
- If you're holding up a tagline as your brand . . .
- If your brand changes yearly . . .
- If your brand only consists of a logo and tagline . . .
- If customers can't quickly identify your brand . . .
- If your brand is only a marketing tool . . .

    . . . then I'm sorry, you don't have a brand.

And then there is my own personal barometer for telling if you are on the right path to brand greatness:

> ## If you're not *feeling* your brand you're *failing* your brand.

At any point in your brand journey stop and check yourself against that simple statement. It is so easy to start congratulating yourself on adhering to the academic rigor of uncovering your brand that you lose sight of why you are embarking on this journey in the first place. The goal is not to look back and say you've gone through the exercise. The goal is to transform your company, excite your customers, inspire your employees, and galvanize your vision. Does that sound like an unemotional process? I truly hope you're emphatically shaking your head no. If not, stop whatever brand process you have going on right now. You're chasing Bland. Not Brand. No harm, no foul. Let's hit rewind and get this back on the right track.

Go back to the basics and begin with your "why" as previously described by Simon Sinek. Your brand is distinctly yours, and as such, it should be evergreen. Don't limit the dialogue to who you are; say what differentiates you instead.

It's hard to step out of the cycle of "what" and shift to "why." One of my favorite examples is with a razor company I worked for. They kept circling around to, "We make razors for people who need a great shave." No matter which way you paint it, that phrase is still "what," because it describes *what* their product is. You have to dig a little deeper to find that "why," or *why* you do the work you do—the driving force behind your decision to take this chance. With that, you'll amplify your own voice and start the process of creating a Craveable Brand.

Sometimes, the best examples of a brand are non-examples of companies failing to live their brands.

Be Your Brand: No More, No Less

The leading brand for women's undergarments is undoubtedly Victoria's Secret & Co. It has multiple clothing lines, tons of media exposure, and an entire fashion show dedicated just to its brand.

Yes, Victoria's Secret (VS) theoretically has a brand that, based on the global recognition and sales over the years, we could be led to believe is a strong brand that would sustain it for years to come. This is how VS articulated its brands: "Brands that Inspire. Empower. Uplift. We don't just sell products . . . we inspire customers around the world with products and experiences that support them on their journey . . . we're committed to fostering a happy, healthy, *and inclusive culture.*"

On paper, VS's brand mission seems spot on. It rings of inspiration, experience, and inclusivity, all of the things you'd want to build a great brand on. But that's as far as its brand mission got: the piece of paper it was written on. The brand preached empowerment and women owning their bodies and sexuality, but from the beginning, it avoided diversity in its marketing. A person could look at ads and images, and see the same body types, races, ethnicities, and appearances. Decades have passed and still, its efforts to diversify are limited.

As recently as November of 2018, the Chief Marketing Officer, Ed Razek, said they had no plans to add larger sizes or transgender models to its lingerie range: "We market to who we sell to, and we don't market to the whole world."[3]

I agree, it's impossible to market to everyone; however, there's a difference between not marketing to everyone and promising empowerment and inclusivity in your brand and failing to deliver. At the time of his comment, 68 percent of American women wore a size 14 or larger—not exactly uplifting to exclude more than half of its potential market.[4] VS has fallen into a cycle I've seen many times before; it states its brand but diminishes the brand to a tagline and some buzzwords. Instead, Victoria's Secret needs to commit to its brand and embody it in *every* decision.

Not every brand is meant to change the world, and that is perfectly fine. The danger for a company is going out and touting your brand's humanitarian commitment when, in reality, you have no intention of delivering on it. That is a far more inexcusable offense to consumers than standing proudly for something better suited to your wheelhouse.

Let your brand celebrate who you are, no matter how small or vain, to the people who embrace you. Victoria's Secret has built an empire based on fantasy. The world needs fantasy and will beat a path to the doorstep of a company that delivers it in the unique way that Victoria's Secret has. But from a brand standpoint, companies run into trouble when their authentic brand tries to stand for more than it is and parade Gisele Bundchen and Mother Theresa down the same runway. That's a recipe for getting your wings clipped. Victoria's Secret has seen a decline in sales and canceled its iconic television runway show, which its CEO claims was due to the show's lack of impact on next-day sales. But the real reasons are more complicated and from my experience, it's likely interwoven in a tale of a brand mismanagement or overreaching.

Squirrels Are Not Your Brand

So how are companies so easily distracted off the path to realizing their own true brand? I think the answer can be found in a very unlikely place.

In the Pixar movie *Up*, a loveable golden retriever named Dug, who has the miraculous power to speak, is constantly interrupting himself by barking "Squirrel" and then tearing off after said rodent in hot pursuit.[5] There are more metaphorical squirrels in our industry to distract you from your brand journey than a thousand Dugs could dream of. The trick is to acknowledge the squirrels and then let them go squeakily on their way. Your job is to keep your eye on the prize. But can you distinguish a squirrel from a brand? And if you saw one, would you go chasing it up the wrong tree?

If you buy into the misconception that a brand is really just a bunch of disparate marketing tools instead of a cornerstone to company-wide change, you will forever be chasing a whole bunch of distracting squirrels up trees that won't lead to your brand.

If all your brand accomplishes is the creation of more marketing efforts, you're going down the wrong path, and you've minimized the brand and its potential impact on the overall company. Your brand should be woven into your entire business. It's not just a list of product attributes, a slew of catchy phrases, or an attempt to engage your audience—all of these are misleading squirrels—your brand is at the heart of your business. I repeat this sentiment because it's crucial to understand this bottom line if you want to create a Craveable Brand.

Some CMOs and similarly data-driven people become convinced that if you unlock a digital buy, a brand will be born of your efforts. Again, you would be drawing a conclusion after only looking at half of the picture. You can analyze the click-through rate, SEO, pay-per-click, and sales, and use that data as a measurement of success—in fact, I encourage it—but don't stop at the data. Without emotional engagement driving the data, you'll only end up watching those numbers decline as customers drop your product or service from one day to the next. Why should they have any loyalty to a company they feel nothing for? You can be just a business to your customers, or you can represent a deeper purpose, inspiring customer loyalty.

Business people can hang on to data like life preservers, but at the end of the day, you need to trust the creatives to do their jobs: emotion-laden engagement and branding.

Some of the mistrust between data-driven people and creatives likely occurs because the idea of branding has become diluted. To be clear, there was always some confusion surrounding what constitutes branding. Even in the beginning, when companies first learned about branding, people would slap on a pretty picture with their business name and call it a brand.

The surge of technology and media, and the replacement of mom-and-pop shops with conglomerate titans has intensified these misunderstandings even more. From the outside looking in, these mega companies appear to be the epitome of great brands; they have the money and influence to be on every laptop, television, and newspaper in the country, all at the same time.

With access to all of the data they could ever need, the titan companies can pay to make sweeping business decisions that reach across the world. But as indestructible and daunting as they may appear to a challenger brand, many of them aren't strong brands at all and, in reality, are ripe to be overtaken. Whoever said that a business can be "too big to fail" hasn't been reading the newspaper. Big companies fail each and every day. Don't be intimidated by your category leader. Size does not equal brand. Quietly build your challenger company around a sustainable brand and be standing strong when the big guy starts to flounder and its customers start jumping over to your highly seaworthy and much more brand-relevant vessel.

In many ways, the lack of brand clarity has allowed for the proliferation and bifurcation of the marketing industry. You have companies like ours, Garrand Moehlenkamp, which places extreme value on analyzing and articulating a company's Craveable Brand and how it's creatively expressed across your whole company . . . and then you have other advertising agencies that place more emphasis on creative disruption, and others still simply pump out swarms of digital ad gnats. There is a considerable gap in the breadth and quality of services here. That line is not a hard and fast one. And there are merits to all approaches depending on what you want for your company. But I have worked for many types of agencies and have experienced more success building brands made of deeper stuff.

If the agency you are working with is only able to deliver style or volume to your company—but no brand substance—you may just be getting a short-term brand-aid that is glossing over a problem that requires a more meaningful solution. Decades ago, a company could misstep and still survive. But now, in the age of accountability, there's too much exposure and too much competition to lose valuable seconds leaving your brand undefined and instead chasing squirrels.

Check Its Pulse: Is Your Brand Alive?

I mentioned this earlier, but it's worth mentioning again: if you're not feeling your brand, you're failing your brand. And you can't feel your brand in a vacuum—aka, the confines of your office space. You need to witness and hear the effect your brand is having on your customers, your employees, and your sales team. Why? Because what you think your brand is communicating to your customers may not be what your customers are *feeling*. It's not enough to sit in your chair and justify your brand to yourself, you need to go out and be a fly on the wall. It's more important to know what people are saying about you when you're not in the room. In fact, maybe one of the best definitions of brand I have ever heard is a quote attributed to Jeff Bezos. It states, "Your brand is what others say about you when you're not in the room." The truth sometimes stings, but it's in that unvarnished truth that we find the raw material to build off of. So, get out and hear it from the horse's mouth, not the hotshot jockey whose salary you're paying.

Do you have a **brand?**

A "no" means there's still work to be done.

	Yes	No
Is your "brand" built on human truths, empathy and creativity?	○	○
Do you feel your "brand" more than you rationalize it?	○	○
Is your "brand" being activated outside of marketing?	○	○
Is your "brand" the lens through which you make every big company decision?	○	○
Does your "brand" fill you and your teams with purpose?	○	○
Does your "brand" embody why you exist, not what you do?	○	○

Trying to capture true, unvarnished, and emotional customer reactions is also why I always prefer qualitative research to quantitative. With qualitative research, you get to keep a pulse on your customers and see those responses firsthand. Body language can tell you as much as what a customer is saying. There are many industry experts who have a bias against focus groups because they believe that group dynamics negatively impact your ability to get pure reads from everybody in the room. And while that can be true, I find that the positives of focus groups outweigh the negatives. You need to go into them with an open mind and sharp focus to read between the lines. As an avid observer of human behavior, I have developed the skill of being able to separate the wheat from the chaff, as they say. I gain powerful insights sitting in focus groups, eating mouthfuls of M&Ms and pretzels.

In many ways, these "behind closed doors" insights will give you the most accurate representation of your brand. Find out what customers and employees truly think of your brand, and you're likely to uncover 1) where your marketing is falling short, and 2) the authentic values of your company that need to be emphasized in your brand. The branding of your company has impacts far beyond you. It will create emotional ripples, intended and unintended. Your brand will steer the direction of those ripples. And unvarnished, public opinion should steer your brand.

A Branded Example

Take a look at Pepsi. Over many decades, it has flirted with capturing its authentic brand. Pepsi came out of the gates hot with the Pepsi Challenge, a national taste test that dared to challenge the supremacy of Coca-Cola, never usurping the top position but sealing a strong second place. Then came "the choice of a new generation," and Michael Jackson set the world, and his hair, on fire. And then it happened—Pepsi fell into the same trap that is tripping up countless brands today.

Pepsi tried to find brand relevance by surfing the waves of all of the latest media trends. It began flooding their social media platforms as if that counted as "the brand." But Pepsi left one thing behind: its emotional connection to their loyal fans. It all came to a head with their ad using Kendall Jenner. Sure, companies use celebrities all of the time to endorse their products. Pitbull endorsed Dr. Pepper, Maroon 5 chose Coca-Cola, and Beyoncé showed up for Pepsi.[6] Most of the time, the ads are a vibrant mix of color and music with a rehearsed moment of a celebrity unwinding as a "relatable" lover of the product. Pepsi, however, wanted something edgy and memorable, and boy, was it memorable.

The culturally insensitive Pepsi ad started off with a call to peace and love, showing demonstrators filling the streets with signs. Then, Pepsi abruptly deviated when Kendall Jenner left the protestors to give one of the cops a soda. This wasn't just a swing and miss by the marketing team; this was a misstep that the world *refused* to forgive, particularly because of the timing.

The commercial was released during the rise of the Black Lives Matter movement and consequent protests against police brutality. To have this celebrity, famous for modeling and reality TV, step across the picket lines and give a cop a Pepsi was so far beyond the scope of Pepsi's brand.

In the wake of the immense anger it stirred, Pepsi pulled the commercial and has remained relatively quiet. In this case, silence was probably the best remedy, rather than trying to actively apologize to resuscitate their image. But where is Pepsi today? Who is it today? I really can't say other than I'm drinking more Coke than Pepsi.

This example isn't to say that businesses can't comment on social issues or support movements; they just need to be movements authentic to their brand. One of our clients, New England Coffee, recognized the crucial nature of staying true to your brand as you weigh into trending cultural topics. The #thankyoubreak was launched in an effort to recognize and thank teachers for how dedicated they are, particularly with the added stress of the pandemic. New England Coffee visited 25 schools, passed out 2,617 free cups of coffee, and managed to capture the nation's attention. People got the added reminder to appreciate their teachers and the continual sacrifices they make, all in the name of education.

New England Coffee could have instead chosen to raise funds for a dog shelter or give out free coffee to a local gym, but the connection between their product and the gesture wouldn't have been in alignment with the authentic brand we had created for them. Six years earlier, we launched New England Coffee's brand platform "Count on every Cup," which not only sought to highlight their consistent 100-year-old roasting process and distinct flavor but also embraced a new emotive mission: "There are people we count on every day, and they count on New England Coffee." And goodness, have we counted on our teachers! Especially during the pandemic. Teachers *are* the backbone of the education system and the majority of them don't get the breaks they need; the pandemic only intensified this. A free coffee endeavor with music and conversation intertwined was a natural step for New England Coffee to recognize and champion our frontline teachers.

Say, New England Coffee had chosen a different recipient for their campaign. Sure, it would still be seen as a kind, giving gesture, but New England Coffe would have missed the opportunity to solidify its values and its brand to customers. If you do misstep, there's always the possibility of recovery, but if and only if you're open and honest about your misstep. If you layer on insincere apologies and don't own up, it's game over.

Adding layers of forced emotion over a company's business practices doesn't make it a brand. Ask yourself: does this action connect to who you are and what you're doing? Does it amplify your emotional resonance? Many companies go through the motions of saying the right thing instead of actually doing the right thing, and customers can see right through this charade; believe me, it won't charm them.

Remember, your brand is a living, feeling thing. It has a personality that either you are portraying, or your customers will for you. You can build your brand as a lifeless list of goals and procedures that elicit enough sales to keep you bumping along, or you can build it as a mission-based juggernaut with an eye on constantly nourishing a better company and a grateful customer base. It's your choice.

A Long-Term Commitment

If you haven't landed on your true brand yet, chances are you will keep switching it out year after year. Without going through the deeply engaging and emotional process of finding your true brand, you are less likely to be committed to it. As the saying goes, "If you don't stand for something, you'll fall for anything." But brander beware. It may be tempting to look at your brand as something you can reset and start from scratch if progress isn't going as you planned. But you don't get unlimited tries to get your brand right—this isn't a video game where you're granted unlimited lives despite brand-building being an adventure. A brand shouldn't be looked at lightly, so you have to be focused and strategic with your efforts.

The way we define the "best" brands isn't about flashing or mirroring cultural trends; longevity is what really matters. Brands require more than flighty attempts—they need consistency in order to build trust and engage customers. True fans of a brand will actively live their lives dedicated to the products that they have the strongest emotional connection with. It's the reason why people have such strong opinions between Coke and Pepsi or Starbucks and Dunkin'. If you take the time to get to know your brand, you'll be rewarded with potentially life-long fandom.

Some of my favorite partnerships are with clients I've had for years. It's not just the camaraderie I cherish, either. No, it's because they're further along in their brand development, so not only have we developed a strong brand vision together, but we also speak the same common brand language by that point. There's no need for translation: I recognize their values, and they understand my practice. With this appreciation, my agency can solve their problems faster and with a greater impact. It's the long-term dedication that builds up the momentum of juggernaut brands.

The first few months of any relationship can be filled with hesitancy and miss-steps, but it's all a part of the process of everyone learning what it means to "live" the brand. It's akin to great sports franchise teams that become dynasties. This kind of success doesn't happen overnight; it's because they all train, learn from losses, and embrace the highs of their wins together. Our shared history with long-term clients allows us to deliver stronger work because we have this extensive, inner knowledge of their brand.

Brand transformation takes courage and time. It takes a firm belief that what your company stands for will always be as important as what you're selling. Great branding cannot be accomplished with a half-hearted commitment. It may be that your brand transformation will roll out over time, but it's important that you see it through to the end. Embracing your brand has the ability to transform every aspect of your company. If you can't clearly see how it will have a transformative power, then you need to dig deeper. The brand is there; you just haven't found it yet.

Your brand is not disposable, so don't treat it as such. It needs to be an intentional, consistent engagement over a period of time to really reap the benefits. Many companies begin their branding journeys and do the initial work, but when it comes to living by the brand's principles, they default to what they know, making that early progress ineffective. This is a disservice to your customers, your employees, and your business.

If you build your brand, creatively express it, and then nourish, nourish, *nourish* it, your company will find its path to greatness. Just be sure to recognize and avoid the signs pointing you down the wrong paths as well. Your true brand will thank you.

Chapter **eight**

Creativity, the Heart of Branding

A brand is a lot like a Formula One race car; it is a finely tuned machine with every piece working in perfect harmony to achieve exceptional performance. After engineering a high-powered brand that sits revving at the starting line, do you just pump any old fuel into it? As with many things, including brands, the old saying, "Sh#% in. Sh@* out," holds true. So what is the fuel that powers all great brands? You want a high-octane premium fuel. For badass brands, that fuel is creativity.

After participating in thousands of creative presentations, I have come to identify two undeniable truths about the role of creativity in building brands. The first undeniable truth is that you cannot create and maintain a strong brand without it. The more creative a brand is, the greater distance it puts between itself and its competitors. "Surprise" and "delight" separate great brands from struggling ones, and if those two characteristics aren't present, you'll fail to elevate your brand above the competition. Creativity and successful branding go hand in hand; there is no escaping it. But don't take my word for It. A recent 2023 article by Delloite resoundingly shows the effect of creativity on business growth.[1]

The second undeniable truth I've come to understand about creativity is that the creative process scares the crap out of people who haven't chosen it as their career path. It takes a brave soul to fully embrace the crunchy process of creatively bringing and keeping a brand alive and vibrant. Why? Because it is not the playground that most of us are intrinsically comfortable playing in. People don't understand it. And when we don't understand something, we don't trust it. But let me assure you, if you commit to defining your company's true purpose and values, the creative process will not be so scary. In fact, it will be downright joyful. So why does the creative process strike fear into the hearts of so many? First, I believe that most business people are very good at leveraging and evaluating the impact of basic business tools such as cash flow, operations, sales, and manufacturing on their business. But it has always been harder for them to evaluate the ROI of creativity.

I have witnessed firsthand the exponential growth impact that creative brand building has had on clients, big and small. Without a doubt, creativity—when applied correctly—is the most powerful business tool available to companies today.

Creative thinking plays an integral role in the early strategic stages of the branding process as you begin to define it. It becomes even more important when leveraged as a business tool, carrying your brand across the finish line to that guarded audience you are trying to connect with. Article after article has shown creativity drives results.

Craveable Brands
actually deliver
hard results

Businesses that focus on brand will consistently outperform the market.

"*2022 saw the fastest rate of brand value growth ever recorded. While financial markets have shown significant swings over the last few years, the value of the world's strongest brands has steadily increased driving customer choice, loyalty, and margins.*" - **InterBrand**

"*Being innovative does pay off. Companies that are marketing and sales innovators are growing at 4.1 percentage points faster compared to lagging companies.*" - **McKinsey**

"*Creativity drives brand success*" with data showing "*67% of highly creative brands achieve above-average organic revenue growth.*" - **McKinsey**

"*Trust is a multiplier: 88% of consumers say that when a company earns their trust it also earns a recommendation to friends and family.*" - **PWC**

"*Selling the brand inside drives results ... When people care about and believe in the brand, they're motivated to work harder and their loyalty to the company increases. Employees are unified and inspired by a common sense of purpose and identity.*" - **Harvard Business Review**

"*Strong brands consistently outperform the market. The world's 40 strongest brands yielded almost twice the total return to shareholders over the course of a 20-year period ending in 2019.*" - **McKinsey**

I have often referred to creativity as the Trojan Horse. Your audience sits just beyond a well-guarded iron fortress built to protect them from the onslaught of advertising messaging targeted at them daily. *But wait, they think to themselves, what is that mesmerizing and beautiful wooden horse that sits just outside the gate? I haven't seen anything that interesting in a long time. Lower the gates! This is worth a second look.*

Congratulations, creativity has gotten you through the first lines of your audience's defense. Unfortunately, this is where many professionals in the marketing industry pat themselves on the back and head back to camp for a celebratory grog. Mission accomplished! Not so fast. Getting through the gates has merely gotten you an audience with a potential customer, who today has the attention span of a goldfish. If what pops out of that Trojan Horse isn't brilliant, swift, and relevant, it will callously be thrust upon the garbage heap of other discarded Trojan Horses that were able to pass through the gates but contained nothing more than what typically pops out of the backside of a horse.

That is the irreplaceable and absolute value of great creativity. It grabs your audiences' attention and then leaves them with a brand message that connects with them on a deep, emotional level. It takes time and skill to creatively express your brand personality so that everyone from customers to employees knows who you are and what you stand for. It's also the single greatest reason that smart marketing agencies could and should command the price tags they do. Brilliant creativity is in short supply. But creativity on any level will still elevate your brand above a boring competitor. The skills needed to produce strategic, attention-grabbing, creative brand work can be achieved by anyone who is willing to take the step of letting their inner creative out. This means giving the rational side of your brain a long overdue vacation and inviting the imaginative and hopeful part to come out and play.

Brand Personality

It may feel uncomfortable at first, but trust me, you have it in you to creatively express your brand like no one else. There are some first basic steps that will help guide your thinking and get you asking the right questions. Such as, what is a brand personality, and do we have one? The answer is yes, and you should meet yours today. Brand personalities—or the way in which you uniquely present your brand's voice and opinions to the world—make brands difficult to mimic. Understanding and defining that personality will lay the foundation for your exciting journey into creatively expressing your brand.

Creatively expressing a brand's personality in a way that is compelling to your customers and motivating to your employees is a daunting task, but don't fret. Are you fun and comical? Empathetic? Proud? Intellectual? That is for you to decide. It's *how* you express and own your personality that matters more than what it is. Be proud of your brand and believe in it: brand personality should be an outward display of your values and the way you see the world. When harnessed correctly, it should feel effortless, authentic, and natural. It offers an opportunity for customers and employees to identify with you on a personal level beyond your product attributes.

We have defined our agency's brand personality as scrappy and nourishing. This wasn't an arbitrary declaration of our personality, rather, we recognized these qualities in the way we consistently operate and work together. We've built our personality around who we are: a mid-size branding agency that services many ambitious challenger brands that will do whatever it takes to grow. Over the years, we have adopted the same industrious energy of our clients for our own. We work with disruptors looking to overtake category leaders ahead of them, and they will take risks to shake up the category for growth. Those are clients we will go to battle with all day long because they understand the disruptive potential of a well-articulated brand and how to strategically apply it for category domination.

If the personality you choose isn't already who you are, you are courting disaster trying to become something you're not. Some companies will want to be the quirky and funny brand attempting eye-catching Super Bowl-type messaging, which can bring about short-term success, but if the heart of your values doesn't necessarily match with the voice you are using in the marketplace, you're missing a huge opportunity. Your brand's personality is a tool that can resonate through your products, people, and communications and rally a following behind you.

Our agency is passionate about leveraging brand for competitive advantage and applying it fiercely and frequently. And it is more important that a company nourishes its customer relationships with frequent brand messaging rather than fixating on a few "perfect" messages. Do not fear being a frequent brand communicator. Not all of your attempts will be gold. Our agency assumes there is always an acceptable level of misses so when they happen we are not deterred. You don't blackball your best friend after they let you down, do you? We are human and mistakes are a given. When it happens, we forgive ourselves, learn fast, and move forward. We remain scrappy in our strategies to deliver and nourish the brands we work with. Our work is never "one and done." It is an ongoing committed process. That is our personality and the way we present ourselves to the world.

Disruption and Creativity

The very nature of creativity is the process of making something that has never been made before. In our industry, perhaps the most quoted book on creativity comes from Jean Marie Dru, the Chairman of TBWA, one of the most celebrated agencies in the world. His book, *Disruption*, (and the handful of sequels it inspired) is about "uncovering the culturally embedded biases and conventions that shape standard approaches to business thinking and get in the way of clear, creative thinking." Dru's approach to disruption is about shattering the set biases and conventions and releasing creativity in the process. Whatever your brand or product represented before, it should be radically different now. To Dru, it was about "spearheading change rather than reacting to it."[2]

Unfortunately, a generation of young, talented creatives in the marketing industry seemed to only read the cover and interpreted the book as a rallying cry to create ideas that "disrupted" at all costs (just getting the Trojan Horse through the gate!). However, Dru's book covered a much larger application of the concept of "creative disruption" for businesses, corporate structures, products, and services. While it was written to be a thoughtful and innovative new way of thinking that could affect all aspects of a company, it became a much more narrowly interpreted call to arms for creative departments across the world to unleash their unbridled creativity at all costs.

I will say this simply and emphatically: you should never disrupt for the sake of disruption. There are thousands of my good creative friends who would disagree with that statement. But I believe a company must always maintain its authenticity, brand personality, and emotionally-relevant message *while* it disrupts. This is where the marketing industry has gone down a rabbit hole. Marketers have interpreted disruption as saying, showing, or creating something crazy that viewers can't help but take notice of. But all you capture when you do this is a single moment of someone's time, someone who just moves on from there without feeling any lasting connection.

True disruption happens when you deeply understand the emotional bias of your audience and tap into that with an idea that speaks uniquely and memorably to their hearts and heads. You can use creativity that may not seem disruptive or crazy at first look, but to the right audience, it strikes a disruptive chord that they can't stop thinking about. Great brands don't overlay an ill-fitting layer of "creative" on top of who they are for the purpose of getting momentary attention. Great brands stay true to who they are and use creativity to express their authenticity in a way that is disruptive to the right audience because it smacks them in the heart, not the face.

Don't Fear the Box

This may seem surprising coming from an award-winning creative, but one of the things I really hate hearing most from a client is "think outside the box!"

This is how that scenario always plays out:

In our first meeting with the client, they want to show their love for creativity and want us to know it. So, they say, "Take the handcuffs off and go for it!" Our agency then goes back to our drawing boards and we let the ideas flow free and unfiltered. There's excitement because this client has given us the freedom that will lead us to our next big creative award. And why not? We were just given a free license to explore the client's brand openly and freely.

Loads of time and money are spent squeezing those creative brains and bringing back something truly brilliant. This is going to be the big one! And then this is where it typically all goes wrong. The client sees all that brilliant work and, after all, your investment in thinking outside the box, all of a sudden, the box gets *a lot* smaller. "Oh, that's not what I thought you'd do.

Could we try doing it this way instead? And by the way, could you use a different color? I hate red."

It's not that I don't appreciate the client's enthusiasm for cutting the creatives loose, but I have found that creatives are at their best when working within a thoughtfully well-defined and tight box (notice, I said thoughtfully). *That* is the challenge that inspires us. Anyone can disrupt for disruption's sake. Strip down naked and run through the halls. Believe me—you will be disrupting but end up in the back of a squad car. Great creatives love to create inside the limitations that other creatives fear to tread. We like to work within a box that sets the parameters for inventive thinking.

This doesn't go for just agencies or contractors you may work with; in-house creatives need these guidelines as well. Even though you may all be united behind your company's core values and brand personality, their perspective as creatives needs to be focused. Clear communication from the outset is a more productive path than just setting your creatives loose to "disrupt" and finding out what that means later.

A great creative mind, Ernie Schenk, who I've had the pleasure of working with for many years, wrote a wonderful book on the subject, *The Houdini Solution*. If you are a creative or are hiring creatives to build your brand, I highly recommend reading it. To get your best work, build smart, insightful, well-defined boxes for them, and then get out of the way for them to do their work.

Collaborate to Create

If your company does decide that it has the resources and the desire to hire an agency and utilize its creative department, the best thing for you to do is trust those creatives. Make them your ally and they will jump through hoops for you. I've worked with every shade of creative under the sun in my thirty-five years, and I've learned a lot about what motivates and demotivates them.

Throughout time, the creative mind has been portrayed as a restless, dark, and lonely place. Sure, many may seem to fit that typecast, but it is a gross misrepresentation of the brilliant talent I have had the honor of working with.

Contrary to popular belief, most creative people crave working with a talented group of people with a shared vision. That loner stereotype is reinforced by mismanagement when managers isolate creative minds from one another. Creatives are hard-wired to produce uniqueness in a world where being unique is seen as frightening and untrustworthy. Quite possibly, the most valued skill I've learned while overseeing creative departments for large international agencies is in creating the right conditions with our clients for creatives to thrive. Creativity should be respected and desired for its transformative powers. The best creatives demand a lot from themselves and will spend an exorbitant amount of their life in pursuit of elusive originality. They don't ask that everyone they partner with will do the same, but they do ask that, in return for their dogged commitment, those partners are, at the very least, not lazy roadblocks. It is much easier to be a destroyer of ideas than a creator of them. Be respectful of the creative process, and honest and thoughtful with your feedback.

Within those conditions, great creatives will give you everything they have because you have proven to be their trusted ally. It is a given that your company's strategy, goals, and operations will continually evolve and morph as you grow, but never stop believing creativity is the fuel that drives the engine for every aspect of your brand and company.

Whatever your brand personality is, be proud of it and believe in it; it has to be honest enough that it drives your brand forward. Your personality will resonate differently for your employees than it will with your customers; we all look at life through different lenses, but the heart of your brand's personality should be the same. It may take a moment for hired creatives to fully tap into the potential of your brand personality, but give it time. Just as it's hard to know someone's full personality as soon as you meet them, you can introduce teams to your brand with an iterative approach. Baby steps. The more authentic and concise your brand personality is, the easier it will be to know and adopt.

Storytelling as a Creative Tool

At the end of the day, the most effective form of communicating your brand is storytelling. Stories have shaped the tenor and trajectory of history ever since the world began speaking to one another. Our collective and individual histories are passed down through storytelling.

We all want to believe that our lives are not simply footnotes at the bottom of the page, but that we are an integral part of the bigger narrative out there, even if it means playing a supporting role in someone else's story. Great brands understand that insight and narrate their story in a way that includes their customers, employees, and leadership in a meaningful narrative that is bigger than all of them.

If I'm an employee and I hear my company's story told in the perfect way, with me as a central character, I'll be more excited to go to work every day. As a customer, I might be more willing to continue buying a product in order to remain the protagonist of that story. And as a business leader, I may be more inspired to drive innovative change in order to evolve and preserve that story where I am a central character. A well-articulated brand will provide the stage for your company's stories to play out. If your company isn't telling captivating stories, then either your brand articulation or the quality of your stories isn't up to par, and it's time to re-evaluate. The good news is that sometimes the inspiration for your stories is right under your nose, or at other times hanging right above your head, which was the case for one of the world's largest insurance providers that came knocking on our door.

I talked before about how we built Liberty Mutual a brand to gain a competitive position against the industry holders, Geico and Progressive. Now I want to zoom out and look at the *story* being told. Liberty Mutual was in a crisis when it came to us for branding help. In the fast-changing world of big insurance, it was seen as a company still holding onto traditional ways and stuck in the past. While Geico and Progressive were re-inventing the category with Geckos, Camels, and Flo, Liberty Mutual was still selling old-school values and at a higher cost. The cost was justified by its passionate responsiveness and responsibility to its policyholders, but most prospective customers didn't stick around long enough to read the bullet points. This left Liberty Mutual with a choice; either it had to compromise its century-old brand values in order to be seen as "cut-rate," or it had to go all-in on its brand. The challenge we faced: find a compelling way to tell its authentic *story*.

The story is what wins people over. It is the "why" that captures your attention and pulls at your heart and mind. As I said earlier, the answer was hanging over our heads, literally. When you walk into the lobby of Liberty Mutual in Boston, carved on the wall above the reception desk is Liberty's mission statement, extolling the virtues of responsibility, the principle the company was founded on. Not as sexy as talking camels, but to my eyes, it was a brilliant shining north star. It was authentic, true, aspirational, and emotional—all of the things missing from most brands today. Our job was to take it and tell Liberty Mutual's story in a way that could resonate more deeply than a green lizard.

With its new brand platform—"Responsibility. What's your policy?"—we didn't just create a new ad campaign, we created a national movement that sprung from Liberty's values and drew a line between those people who proudly took responsibility for their lives and actions and those that didn't.

"The Responsibility Project," our online site that housed stories of people and organizations doing the right thing, became so popular that some days it was drawing more online traffic than Amazon! We had hit a nerve in this country with great storytelling, and Liberty was the hero of that story. Not only did the campaign help Liberty to re-establish and remain at the top of the insurance food chain, but it also won a Cannes Lion, our industry's top creative award. In this case, it wasn't Liberty's brand that was broken, it was how its brand was telling its story that needed a creative refresh. Again, that's the power of creative storytelling.

A crucial part of communicating your brand story is ensuring that you are communicating it in the right voice. With the appropriate voice, you can have your messaging resonate to the core of your customers and your employees. Remember, it's called marketing communications for a reason. To effectively communicate, you need to speak to your audience in a voice that resonates with them and makes them want to continue to listen, or even better, communicate back. Your brand voice will be directed by your brand personality. What you have to say is important, but so is how you say it and how it will be received and remembered. Is your voice empathetic, forceful, encouraging, angry, or comedic? It could be any of these. What is important is that your voice is an authentic representation of your brand. It's the voice that you believe will deeply connect with the needs of your customers and employees. When you wield your authentic brand voice to tell your story with conviction and passion, people will listen. When people stop listening, either your brand is off or you've lost your voice. Companies need to look beyond the strategic functionality of their departments and really see the people in them who are on the receiving end of your brand story. Each of those individuals has their own perspectives and desires to be a part of something bigger. Some of those people will be an internal audience and many will be external. But your brand story needs to resonate with them all. The same brand story can be told a little bit differently to best capture the subtle differences of each of your intended audiences. Your brand is a book that reveals itself over many chapters. When a brand story is told in a compelling and engaging way, it can promote internal alignment and external devotion simultaneously. It was Shakespeare who said, "All the world's a stage and all the men and women merely players." Make your brand part of a great story and give your people starring roles in it. We all appreciate a little limelight.

Boring is Bad. Period.

Saying you're being creative is one thing, but are you actually executing that creativity? There's a timeless litmus test for this: *Is it boring?*

Nothing hurts like being told you are boring. But get comfortable with using that concept as your barometer. Make boring your mortal enemy. It is the kiss of death to you and your company. It's a splash of cold water and the harsh measure of your uniqueness and your relevance to the greater world. To put it bluntly, if your brand is boring, well, then you are dead or dying. You cannot ever make a good excuse for being boring. For your brand to have any hope of being beloved by many, it has to be a standalone aspect of your company that sets a new bar. If you're simply following trends without a unique spin, subversion, or interpretation, I'm afraid you are inherently boring. The antidote to boring is creativity. Take a minute to reflect on the questions below if you have a hunch that your brand or brand messaging is boring:

- Have you seen it before? *If so, it's boring.*
- Did it make you feel something? *If not, it's boring.*
- Are you explaining more than high-fiving? *If so, it's boring.*
- Are people excitedly talking about it? *If not, it's boring.*
- Does it give you a new sense of purpose? *If not, it's boring.*
- Do some people absolutely hate it? *If not, it's boring.*
- Does it make your competition rethink its strategy? *If not, it's boring.*
- Do your customers want to make ads for you? *If not, it's boring.*

In truth, I think you should be *more afraid* of being boring than fully embracing creativity as your company's new superpower. Your brand's personality will shine through with even a lackluster attempt at creative marketing, but something boring doesn't even get you in the conversation. Save your money. If your brand's core values and brand personality stay core to your initial efforts, then take the leap of faith into creativity. You won't fail. Create something new that connects with both your employees and your customers.

Do yourself and your company a favor: embrace the uncomfortable process of creation and revoke boring's building keycard. It will only feel uncomfortable for a while, but the long-term benefits to your company will last for decades.

Chapter nine

If you Brand it, They Will Come

Today, the people your company is trying to reach have a genetically advanced superpower passed down from their ancestors. It's a highly tuned shield developed to filter out ad noise pollution and bullsh*t. For centuries, companies have been trying to get the attention of potential buyers. As the years have passed and the number of companies has multiplied, so has the massive cloud of ad noise hanging over all of our heads waiting for us to breathe it in. Today, being constantly tethered to the internet and our devices, there's a never-ending deluge of messages and information coming through a myriad of screens. It's the price we all pay for that free and amazing online experience.

As a survival measure, all of us have developed a fine-tuned internal radar and filtration system that protects us from being completely overrun by all of this marketing messaging. Companies saw this coming, but instead of evolving their approach, they doubled down on putting out more and more targeted messages in an attempt to keep the audience's attention. The world's attention span has continued to shrink. And in response, marketers have been driven to create smaller, faster bite-sized digital messages that attempt to shoot through the tiniest of attention gaps and worm their way into our brains. Instead of going the route of developing better messaging that respects people's time and intelligence, the industry has instead gone with inundating them with even more annoying "adlets," constantly assaulting our senses like a swarm of gnats.

This not only doesn't work, but it's insulting and disrespectful. It's a dead-end effort that's akin to screaming into a void. Adding *more* messages is not the answer; you need to improve the limited messages you produce. How do you do this? *It begins by looking creatively inward first and excavating your brand.*

Dig, Don't Dance

Pull out your compass, hammer, and pickaxe and set aside the urge to jump immediately into flashy marketing tactics that aim to stun and stupify. First, you will need to excavate the core values at the heart of your company. The best brands are built on the true purpose of the company and, as such, shouldn't be manufactured to fit trends. While the world and consumers are continuously moving targets that you must be aware of and track, your brand should always shoot straight from the heart. Only then will you connect and "win."

Your marketing tactics can adapt to the trends, but your brand truth needs to be a constant and reliable foundation. As brand nourishers, we aren't there to create a brand for our clients; instead, we articulate the truths already present in the company. It's almost impossible to create *something* meaningful from *nothing* but the good news is that companies are built on values, even if they aren't aware of it or are too close to see it. Sometimes it's better, and it can save you time and money in the long run, to introduce an outside agency perspective like ours since we're unfamiliar with any existing politics and biases of the company. We can see what the current brand is with fresh eyes and identify what messaging is being conveyed to their audience versus what the company *thinks* is being communicated. And then help lead your team in the "big dig" for your true brand.

Whether you choose to work with outside specialists for this crucial task or take it on yourselves, this phase comes down to honesty. You have to honestly 1) trust the people who are tasked with this work and 2) be willing to challenge your notion of what your company stands for today.

Determine Your Core Values

If you can't sit down now and jot down 3-5 core values that your business is built on, then prepare for a reality check. A company is unsustainable without values and you need to define some immediately.

When mining for distinct brand truths, think of them as diamonds in the rough. And many times they are just that: rough. I care more that the brand truths are authentic and unique to your company than them being perfect when they are unearthed. It's our job, yours *and* mine, to polish the brand truths to a clear, multi-faceted gem that can service your company on a myriad of levels. The process of mining the most salient raw material from your company and then creatively expressing them is intended to inspire exponential growth through brilliant messaging and internal restructuring of thought and process. Words on paper can be very compelling, obviously, but until those words are brought to life through creative expression, they remain an idea and not a living brand. Creativity brings brands to life for companies, customers, employees, and the world.

Perhaps one of the biggest challenges for clients in the brand excavation phase is momentarily pausing to look inward even when challenges are advancing at them head-on. Reflecting on where your company has come from is necessary to gather insights to better face the challenges of tomorrow. I can tell when we work together that it feels counter-intuitive for most hard-driving executives, who are only focused on the road ahead, to take a beat and look in the rearview mirror to examine where they've come from. But without that honest assessment of who they are, companies end up reinventing the wheel daily based on the challenge du jour. That approach is an exhaustive and unproductive path to brand building.

Creating brand truths that can't be tampered with goes back to ensuring that you are building them off of truths that are undeniable. They are not random, subjective ideas that come to you in the spur of the moment; I'm asking you to dig deep into the highly personal qualities that you see in your company. *This* is what is defendable. *This* is where you'll find the conviction to withstand change and come out on top. If you look inward and don't feel that conviction, then your supposed core values can, and probably should, be debated and argued. I'd even say you can trash them. Without an emotional reaction or a compelling quality, those values are fluff.

Your "boots on the ground" employees will oftentimes have a better understanding of the core values simply because they engage with them every day. It hurts to hear, but sitting behind that big desk sailing at 50,000 feet can isolate you, the leader, from the core of your company. Connecting with the workers and founders of the company through in-depth interviews will reveal the characteristics that distinguish your brand.

This isn't a rush-to-the-finish-line effort though. If you re-launch your brand and the core values are disingenuous or off-base, the repercussions from customers and competition will be swift and brutal. If you launch an inauthentic brand that customers sniff out and drag through the streets, you can't crawl your way back into their favor anytime soon, so keep that red carpet rolled up until the brand truly embodies your defined core values. Until you *feel* you have them.

Cultivate a Compelling Mission Statement

A mission statement is your chance to capture the interest—and potential loyalty—of consumers and prospective employees alike. Where I see clients go wrong is that they use mission statements as a kind of internal memo or measure of standard. Think about the root of the word; it takes grit and tenacity to go on a mission. The very word invokes images of James Bond saving the world or of a thread-dressed person traveling long distances to a place of worship. James Bond's missions weren't a list of "honey do" items for around the house. They were ambitious with a touch of danger thrown in for kicks! A mission statement should be that inspiring; it needs to be the BIG promise you're making to your customers, yourselves, and dare I say it, the world! This is the first story of your brand that will inspire a thousand stories. So it better be one great story.

The application of your values acts as the thesis of your mission statement: how will you do the work in a way that benefits customers and inspires them to care about your business?

For a while, the outdoor clothing company Patagonia confused the difference between a company's what and why. This is a pretty common occurrence. Previously, their mission statement was "to build the best product, cause no unnecessary harm, use business to inspire and implement solutions to the environmental crisis." This isn't actually a mission statement, but rather a business directive—a strategic approach to how Patagonia operates as a company and makes its products. Will that get anyone jumping out of bed raring to get to work? Doubtful.

A great mission statement, however, is a call to action. It inspires the company to want to be better, to do better, and to deliver better because when it does, the company reaps emotional, as well as financial, returns on its effort. We all want purpose and to feel like what we are doing matters, even if it's "just" shopping. A thoughtful and emotionally articulated mission statement is the blueprint to that purpose, as seen in Patagonia's new mission statement, "We're in business to save our home planet."[1] Wow! That is a mission statement that inspires change. So much so that the owner and his family gave the company away to a non-profit organization that will commit all its proceeds to fighting the environmental crisis. Thank you, Patagonia!

While other aspects of building out your brand, like outbound marketing, internal operations, and recruiting, need to be crafted with time and money as considerations, writing your new mission statement relies on just one thing: you and your team. I will say that regardless of your size and goals, your newly-minted brand, core values, and mission statement should be immediately implemented into your daily efforts. There's already been too much of a delay and you don't want to keep your company's future, its customers, and the world waiting!

Brand Platforms; Don't Call It a Tagline!

When I sit new clients down and ask them to walk me through their values and mission statements, I'm quite often given their very inwardly focused mission statement or their most recent tagline. (Sometimes, I get nothing at all!) That's obviously not the starting place I'm looking for and it once again reveals the confusion and misinformation that surrounds branding.

First, as we discussed, your **mission statement** is a declarative, long-form statement that is a call to action for your company. It is an enduring promise and all-encompassing of the company's core values. It should give you goosebumps every time you read it.

A **tagline**, however, is a short pithy phrase that's *related* to your brand, but most often not your brand. And that's a problem. In lieu of articulating their true brand, many companies will default to a tagline as their brand.

But usually what they've created is just a catchy phrase often equated with a product feature—think "Tastes great, less filling" (Miller Lite) or "The milk chocolate that melts in your mouth, not in your hand." (M&Ms). Were these brilliant taglines that worked? Yes, but what if that short catchy line could feature your product and your mission all in one neat package? Spoiler alert, it can! And it's called a **brand platform.**

Now many marketing pundits will say that I am splitting hairs here in trying to parse out the difference between a *tagline* and a *brand platform*—they do indeed look alike and are used in the same way—but without clearly defining the difference between the two, it is very easy to head down the wrong path. Taglines are most often short-lived, pun-filled, marketing-centric creations meant to button up a campaign thought. That is why many people still call them "campaign buttons."[2] Cute . . .

In contrast, a brand platform, while it is short, catchy, and can wrap up a campaign, also serves as the inspirational direction of a company, why it exists, and who it exists for. That is a lot to expect from a few words! But you must demand it and keep chipping away at it until you feel it in your bones. Again, think "America Runs on Dunkin'."

Tagline or Brand Platform?
Know the Difference.

Taglines are one trick ponies used to wrap up marketing campaigns, *brand platforms* galvanize and shape your company's future.

Brand Platforms ⟶ **Taglines**

Nike: "Just Do It."	**KFC:** "Finger lickin' Good."
Apple: "Think Different."	**Folgers:** "Good to the last drop."
Dove: "Real Beauty."	**Hilton:** "For the Stay."
Avis: "We Try Harder."	**Time Warner:** "Enjoy better."

I see many companies who start off doing the work to excavate their brand, lose steam or focus, and then, exasperated, they jump straight to a tagline so they can wrap things up and get on with it. I have to emphasize this: do not rely on a tagline built for your marketing campaign to act as a substitute for your brand. A brilliantly articulated brand, founded on your evergreen core values, can inspire endless marketing campaigns for your company. However, a tagline created for an ad campaign, but masquerading as your brand, can outlive its usefulness once a campaign has run its course.

There's too much at stake and too much competition to expect a catchy marketing tagline to perfectly encapsulate your brand long-term. You are a growing company, one that probably doesn't have a high enough marketing budget that would require a catchy tagline even if that's what you wanted. So why waste time investing in a tagline? A brand platform will not only serve as a way to inspire your marketing efforts, but it will also concurrently inspire your employees, your vision, and your operations, and, best of all, it will grow sales.

Your company could continue to get by on flashy tactics and quality products for a short while, but without a defined brand, your progress will be inconsistent and unpredictable. This is where a brand platform can be your company's north star.

If you're a fan of J.R.R. Tolkien's *Lord of the Rings*, hang onto your hat. The brand platform is akin to "one ring to rule them all." It is an all-encompassing (and inescapable) concept, and it is bigger than the individual components of your company. Your brand platform is the "one ring" that gives meaning and direction to all other aspects of your company and its marketing efforts. Yes, it can—and should—do all of that.

In my experience, most companies have too narrow of a view of what a brand is. They only seem to think of a brand as it pertains to their marketing effort, thereby failing to look at the bigger picture. There's a lot of rigor that goes into defining a brand because of the power it can hold when deployed for good. At my agency, we establish this mindset by asking our clients to consider their brand as a catalyst for improvement in all aspects of their business.

Craveable Brands Don't Live Separately from Sales Activation

The Craveable Brand approach accelerates short-term sales and long-term brand building concurrently.

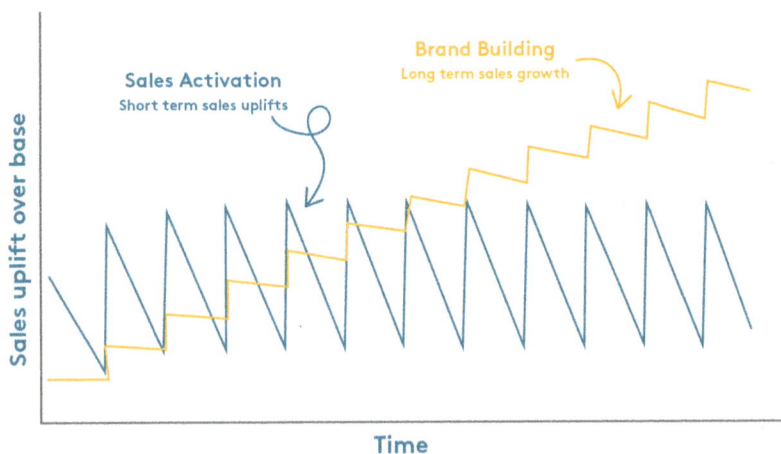

Sales Activation
Short term sales uplifts

Brand Building
Long term sales growth

Sales uplift over base

Time

Source: The Long and the Short of It Binet & Field 2013

It goes beyond a mission statement. Where a mission statement is a promise to the customer, a brand platform is a thoughtful, declarative statement of intent that exemplifies a company's vision for its customers and its larger impact on the world.

This becomes your company's launching platform for all future brand initiatives and marketing tactics. As you proceed, consider how each move you make supports the vision/statement and ask these questions:

- Does it align with your core values?
- Does it represent all aspects of your company?
- Is it motivational to your employees?
- Is it true to your internal personality?
- Does it differentiate you from your competitors?

As a means of further illustrating the difference between a tagline and a brand platform, I have a story from one of our small but mighty clients that you'll find in the mountains of New Hampshire. Don't think for a second that just because it's off the beaten path its presence isn't felt around the world. Hypertherm is the world's largest manufacturer of plasma cutters and other industrial cutters. These are not your mothers pinking shears—these machines cut the steel beams and parts that go into building skyscrapers, bridges, and tractors.

Hypertherm's handy work is splashed across the landscape all over the world. It's big, important work. Hypertherm is a great company that is 100 percent employee-owned and driven by brilliant engineers. When we first started working with Hypertherm, I asked the team, as I usually do, "Why does this company exist?"

And in response, they pointed to their tagline hanging boldly on the wall: *CUT WITH CONFIDENCE*. As far as taglines go, it wasn't a bad one. But it was obviously written from an engineer's perspective, and it didn't carry the juice to change an entire company.

After an interview phase where we talked with the customers who handled these cutters, we realized that beyond the task of cutting metal, these cutters saw themselves as rugged creators shaping the infrastructure of the world. Now *that* is bigger than cutting. Not surprisingly, this same expansive vision was shared by employees, leadership, and OEMs. They just needed a simple yet powerful articulation of this mutual vision. In two words, we were able to capture it: "Hypertherm. Shaping Possibility."

With those two words, we expanded its focus from engineering a cutting product to one of a company proudly shaping the horizon and the future. That phrase not only embraced its role as a leader in cutting but also in employee ownership, visionary engineering, and championing its end users. Those little words have shifted how Hypertherm has evolved as a company. It's a critical example of the difference between a tagline and a brand platform. Your brand platform leaves nothing up to chance because its existence draws a line in the sand. There's no more confusion about who you are, why you do what you do, and what you'll deliver. It is the compass of your entire company, so be sure to treasure it and consult it daily.

I always return to Dunkin' Donuts as an example and that's because it exhibits my approach to branding so well. From a purely analytical lens—no ego involved—the company's brand has been virtually indelible since my team and I got in and defined it. Dunkin' has been sold twice, has had six different CMOs, and it grew fast; I'm talking 300 stores in 2004 to nearly 3,000 in 2022. That averages 150 new stores built per year. And if you look at Dunkin's history, the exponential growth didn't occur until we launched "America Runs on Dunkin'" in 2006. We made Dunkin' a national brand that could outlast the change in leadership many times over. The Dunkin' brand platform was airtight and has remained constant because it's a true reflection of the brand's core; it's heart. Without a heart, an organism fails, and a company is no exception.

The journey to articulating your brand truths, and then betting the farm on them in the form of a brand platform, are acts of courage in my mind. But it is that type of courage that will lead to the exponential growth that few companies ever achieve. It's like when Houdini used to have the audience inspect the water tank, locks, and chains before he was submerged headfirst in the tank only to miraculously escape the chains. *That's* the reaction we want from our clients when we reveal their brand for the first time. Ta-da!

Chapter ten

This Changes Everything.

Your Brand Tool Box

I recently bought a new electric lawn care system that features every kind of lawn tool you can use for your yard: a weed trimmer, chainsaws, a snowblower, a lawn mower, etc. The beauty of the system is that it's powerful enough to cover all of my lawn care needs. But what's most impressive is that every tool runs flawlessly off of the same powerful battery to power a system that handles every aspect of manicuring a beautiful yard. As game-changing as it is, I'm not here with a lawn care advertisement; instead, I want you to think about your brand toolbox in the same way that I admiringly look at my new lawn care system. "Wait, what is a brand toolbox?" you may be asking yourself.

A brand toolbox is the marketing equivalent of a neatly packaged lawn care system. Your company utilizes many tools across your system to succeed; tools like your vision and values, employee benefits, products, social media, company causes, trade shows, etc. And at the heart of all of those tools should be your brand, powering up meaning, clarity, and vision. If you have a faulty brand battery—or worse, no brand at all!—most of those business tools will be underpowered, and their limited function will reduce the overall success of the entire system. And your yard, aka your company, will be a grubby lawn full of weeds.

That is quite simply how the brand toolbox works for our clients. Each toolbox we create is powered by a very compelling and unique brand (and brand platform) at its core, but how it is utilized to supercharge every aspect of their business is the same. That said, can we plug any brand into a brand toolbox and call it a day? Absolutely not. A brand with that kind of multi-tasking ability has to be engineered from the very beginning to allow it to work at that capacity. No ordinary brand will do.

Growing Craveable Brands means Rallying an Entire Organization around a Common Purpose

A Craveable Brand unites an organization, ultimately shaping company culture. It guides actions, sets priorities and creates efficiencies that simplify decision making and amplify growth.

GROWTH STRATEGIES

OPERATIONS & FINANCE

EMPLOYEE ENGAGEMENT & RETENTION

CUSTOMER EXPERIENCE

SALES & MARKETING

TALENT, TOOLS & PARTNERS

R&D/ PRODUCT

Creating a Multi-Tasking Brand
(aka, a Craveable Brand)

If you ask most CMOs and company owners how they define their brand, they are most likely to begin talking about it in terms of their marketing and communications strategy. In doing so, they are unknowingly limiting their company's potential. To continue with the lawn system metaphor—old news I know, but I really like this metaphor—their brand is no longer the one battery powering their whole system; it is just powering one tool. Don't get me wrong, marketing is a very important tool that needs a great brand at its core. But if you knew that you could have a "multi-tasking brand" for the same investment of time and money that it takes you to create a single-use marketing brand, why would you ever settle? I'm here to say that many very smart marketing professionals are making this compromise every day.

It's a tragedy, but I understand where the confusion stems from. As I mentioned earlier, our own industry has to take much of the blame for confusing the definition and role of a brand. The continuous cacophony of marketing blasts only adds to the noise and confusion for consumers, with organizations "yelling" to get people's attention.

The companies that do a great job of branding, such as Dove or Dunkin', explicitly lay out how their brand powers not only their marketing and communication strategies, but every aspect of their company. It's clear to the customers that adore them and their employees who love working for them that their brands permeate every aspect of how they do business. They're clear proof that a brand can transform and inform your entire company. And here are some of those ways your brand can affect your company beyond marketing:

- Your mission statement and core values.
  - *This is your emotional line in the sand.*
- Your logo.
  - *Nike and all that little swoosh have come to signify.*
- Your corporate causes.
  - *Your customers care how you care.*
- Your brand identity.
  - *Your visual identity speaks for itself.*
- Your customer service.
  - *There's customer service and there's Ritz Carlton.*
- Your operations.
  - *To talk the talk and keep walking the walk.*
- Your social media.
  - *Keep yourself out there and let your brand shine.*
- Your products.
  - *Your "what" (product) supports your "why" (brand).*
- Your employees.
  - *Don't just give them a job. Give them purpose.*

At the center of all of these brilliantly executed initiatives powering them to greatness is a single, compelling, and well-articulated brand. As you can see, a brand is a foundation where not only your marketing and communications grow, but it's also a necessary cornerstone for internal operations and external engagement as well. Each tool works best for a specific problem, but together they create a uniform messaging system.

To demonstrate an example of a multi-tasking brand, I will share a recent rebranding effort that we created with our wonderful new client MaidPro, a franchised cleaning service. MaidPro came to us with a simple request to help it clearly define its brand so that it could accelerate growth with new franchisees and customers. This was a company that had a superior product, great leadership, and energetic franchisees. The leadership team knew that there was a huge opportunity to differentiate the company from a crowded competitive landscape on a brand level. After our first meeting with them, we were convinced it could achieve this as well.

As we do with all clients, we first interviewed Maid Pro's own franchisees, leadership team, and executives. We then conducted a research study of existing and potential customers to gather insights to help us build the new Maid Pro brand and reinforce its story.

From our internal Maid Pro research, we learned that this company was dedicated to go the extra mile to better service for its clients. The franchisees were deeply connected with their clients and focused on delivering a higher level of customer service. The cleaning processes included an exhaustive 100-point checklist of services to complete before a house was considered "clean." That's a commitment to quality! And MaidPro's cleaning professionals were the best in the industry.

Our customer research showed that customers who used cleaning services were doing so for very emotional reasons as well as practical. On an emotional level, a clean house was validation of their abilities to maintain a happy home. It gave them a sense of pride and, most importantly, a sense of peace. Deep peace. While our research showed that any level of house cleaning brought joy and calm to homeowners, it also showed us that a thoroughly cleaned home, a MaidPro deep clean, brought measurably more calm and peace of mind. In these chaotic times, who doesn't want the deepest peace of mind money can buy? This insight led to the articulation of MaidPro's new brand platform: "Cleaning is deeper with MaidPro."

It's memorable, a promise of superior service and superior feelings of satisfaction for their customers. It also lays out a north star for the company and its employees to build new services around and indicates how the company should interact with its customers. "Cleaning is deeper with Maid Pro" became the galvanizing idea that married the internal company research with our customer findings. It speaks not just of Maid Pro's commitment to a deeper level of clean for its clients, but it also conveys the deep emotional feelings the brand promotes with its customers. When your home is clean, you feel that sense of peace, and the deeper the clean, the deeper the peace. Hence, "cleaning is deeper." As we apply this brand platform to franchisee development, it takes on a new meaning.

Maid Pro has multiple programs in place for new franchisees and its commitment to its franchisees goes deeper than its competitors with a Cleaning University, franchisee support, and ongoing training. If I'm a potential franchisee and I hear that MaidPro is driven by the belief that "Cleaning is deeper with Maid Pro," I know that cleaning means more to them and that they take their commitment to their clients and franchisees very seriously. It's a very good impression to make.

But a brand's impact doesn't end there. It is designed to be impactful across the company by being able to affect other aspects like their charitable giving. When cleaning is deeper to you, it means you are more deeply concerned with how the brand can make a lasting impact on the world through its actions. Maid Pro provides free cleaning to people going through hard times to raise their spirits and give them a fresh start. This shows deep concern. Or its employee recruitment strategy, which focuses on forging deeper relationships with its cleaners by making them part of a brand they are proud to work for with benefits that are more deeply rewarding. The value Maid Pro can extract from its new brand is limitless. As it should be.

Brand Strategy: A Blueprint for Growth.

While you may think you want to put as many brand tools in your brand toolbox as possible, I would caution you against it. Diving once more into my lawn care analogy, not every yard is the same. Just because you now have a brand platform that can amplify every aspect of your business doesn't mean you should. (If you don't have a tree in your yard, do you need a tree trimmer?) You need to look at your company's business goals and have a plan for which brand tools to include in your toolbox.

While the toolbox is the repository of creative assets that will be utilized across your company, your **brand strategy** is the strategic blueprint that guides which parts of your business your brand toolbox should amplify to achieve your business goals. Your brand strategy is unique to your company and will be shaped by your business goals, vision, budgets, competitive landscape, product mix, etc.

Here is where your left brain can get its mojo going prior to the big handoff to the right brain. The more clearly you understand your company's long-term opportunities and related initiatives, the more assured you will be in crafting a brand strategy that will assist in helping you achieve all of your long-term goals. Narrow-minded brands are created by narrow-minded practitioners who set the brand bar too low. If you come in knowing the full extent of the Herculean task ahead of your brand, you will naturally expect more of it. And you will judge it accordingly. Be ambitious for your brand and demand it of your company and your agency.

Think of your brand strategy as a triage plan. For our agency's part, we act as a specialist taking the vitals of your company. We ask about pain points and history (brand excavation), do a visual assessment (our business analysis), and then determine the most advantageous course of treatment. We act decisively in determining where brands will, and will not, have the greatest impact.

The goal here is to isolate the biggest areas of potential opportunity for our clients. With this plan in place, we hold a weekly status call with our client to discuss how the newly polished brand is being received by the marketplace and customers and the overall marketing efforts. As we mentioned earlier, the areas that we choose to apply our branding efforts first will vary with each client.

This Changes Everything

Growing up, there was an old jingle for a margarine company that I can still remember today. It was sung in a chirpy female voice and went: "Everything's Better with Blue Bonnet on it!" That jingle is what runs through my mind when I think about how companies should view their branding efforts.

Without a doubt, everything's better with branding on it. But again, most people, including very smart business professionals, don't have an idea of how a brand can transform other aspects of their company beyond marketing. The possibilities are endless of course, but as an example, here are just a few of the key areas where you can activate your brand to great effect: operations, products and services, customers, employees, and charitable causes.

Operations

Let's start really big. If you can get your head wrapped around something as ambitious as transforming your whole operations through brand, the rest might seem simple by comparison.

"How does my brand influence the way my company is set up and run?" It's a tough question that I will answer very simply: If you have a brand that you and your customer are bonding over, then structure your company around it and that bond will grow.

If Nike never became *Nike* and just stayed with pumping out running shoes, it may have had a good run (pun intended) until the next innovator made them better or cheaper. But as a brand, Nike evolved to stand for more than just sneakers. It became the voice of humanity realizing its potential through athletic endeavors. How could your operations not change to deliver on a promise that ambitious? It has to. Yes, your brand too can be crafted to have that level of impact on how your company operates.

When we pitched and won Toys "R" Us, we pitched with a new brand that required them to not only re-invent their marketing but also to invest in a restructuring of their operations as well. An architect would go in and change the interior of their retail stores, making it like a clock ticking through the age groups of their different young buyers. The products would be positioned along this new circular customer journey to coincide with the growth of a child's development, with certain toys kept in certain age sections. At the center, there was a big whimsical clock that said "Time for Childhood." Its new brand platform. It was the perfect layout for a toy store trying to give meaning back to the importance of physical playtime throughout childhood and move away from its existing "plastic by the pound" model.

It's a seemingly inconsequential change, but this change to the operation side of Toys "R" Us would have reinforced the brand and brought to life its key focus on child development through play. Much like a child, you have to use your imagination to take your brand and run with it. I dare say it would have saved Toys "R" Us from their unfortunate demise.

Products and Services

Innovation is good, but I believe innovation for the sake of innovation can be an endless hamster wheel of aimless energy if it isn't being focused by your brand. Customers don't want a hodgepodge of products; they want a consistent, branded experience that is supported by innovation.

Apple doesn't capitalize on its popularity by selling trendy products like sneakers or bags: why? Because neither is a natural fit for their brand: Simplicity, Humanity, and Creativity. *Think Different*. It would be a stretch to sell those products even if some audiences would still buy the stuff out of brand loyalty. It's not a good fit and we can all see that.

The same is true for your business. Instead of making products that simply aim to be faster, easier, or cheaper to manufacture, reflect again on the relationship you want with your customers. Are you looking for quantity over quality? Do you want to handle endless customer complaints by shaving off a few thousand dollars with the easy way out? I think not. So take the time to make products you can be proud of, that nurture what you stand for, and ones that are actually influenced by your brand and values.

Customers

When you think about how your brand relates to your customer, think about it this way: Your brand *is* your relationship with your customer. It is the emotional pact that connects you and provides the voice and personality that makes you more than just a product to them.

Each and every touchpoint with your customer should be seen first through the lens of how your brand can help you build on that special relationship. And guess what, the stronger the relationship, the more likely it is that customers will do business with you. It won't be an obligation; they'll *want* to do business. It is easy to let the whole focus of your business be on getting more sales. But, if you fail to look beyond the sale and to the potential customer, you're likely falling short and not meeting their expectations. Your brand is what will inspire more than a one-time buy, so by using your branded language and attitude, you can build a strong relationship with customers.

I know that, initially, this can all sound a bit unpredictable and messy, as relationships often are. But I can promise a happy, connected, engaged customer is what will keep your sales rolling in. Instead of "happy wife, happy life," think, "happy buyer, sales go higher."

Employees

This brings me to one of the most important components of any business: your employees. Your brand has to be embraced, from the top leadership position down through your employees. Uninspired or unsatisfied employees will lack motivation. That's why so many service jobs, such as food service, have a high turnover rate. Now, your company may not have the startling 75 percent turnover rate the restaurant industry boasts, but that doesn't mean your business isn't suffering behind the scenes.[1]

I'm here to say that you don't need a dramatic pay increase or luxurious health benefits to keep employees happy: simply defining and incorporating your brand and values can make a significant difference in employee retention. People want to be inspired; they want to feel like their work matters and they want to go home at the end of the day pleased by their efforts and the efforts of the company. So be the boss and business that represents more than a paycheck and you'll find that not only will your employees stay in the job longer, they'll be happier and your business will blossom as a direct result. That inspiration to your employees is your brand.

Richard Branson is quoted as saying, "Clients do not come first. Employees come first. If you take care of your employees, they will take care of the clients."[2] With a brand that inspires both employees and customers, you open up a world of possibilities for positive engagement.

Charitable Causes

Maybe more than at any time in our history, customers are choosing to buy from companies whose causes align with their own. When it comes to branding and philanthropy, it's not so much centered on how much you are giving back to the planet, or who you are giving to, but rather *why* you are giving back at all. The reasons why you are giving back need to be clearly aligned with your company values. Why? Because if they aren't, you run the risk of appearing disingenuous.

The world loves to embrace companies with a social conscience, almost as much as they love tearing down companies who are pretending to care. Nothing can bring emotional gravitas to your brand like a well-executed philanthropic strategy that springs from your brand values. And nothing can bring it down faster than half-heartedly supporting a cause for the PR opportunity. Be sure you deeply believe in why you're giving and have those reasons spelled out for your leadership team.

Planning for Success

These are just a handful of the places where a brand can be implemented in your company to give more clarity, meaning, and direction to your efforts. As you begin to successfully implement your brand in a few places, you will find that branding becomes addictive. The more you see what it can do, the more you'll want to use it and fall deeper in love with it every time you do.

As we mentioned earlier, our branding agency, Garand Moehlenkamp, has a scrappy and nurturing brand. We carefully infuse that brand into all aspects of our agency. We hire people who are self-motivated, engaged problem solvers, and are able to self-manage. They're inspired to disrupt the industry, be creative, and grow clients' businesses. That's the perfect person I want to work with every day.

In terms of our "products" and operations, we make sure to detail a thorough plan that's specific to each client, and we have one person whose sole job is to sit in on weekly client meetings, directing our energy and focus to the right places. Finally, we ensure that for every task, we are more ambitious than our clients. Clients spend their whole week plugging holes and putting out fires, so we're that outside help that can take a step back, rationally analyze the problem, and enact a creative solution. Our brand is evident at each level of our business and with our toolbox in tow, we make our mark.

With a strong brand powering your toolbox, you're on the right track to grow your company by amplifying every department and initiative.

Not Just Any Brand. It's Your Brand.

As my agency strategically collaborates with clients like MaidPro, Shipley Do-Nuts, and New England Coffee to excavate and articulate their true brand, we work under the assumption that its ultimate value to clients has to be nothing less than transformational across all aspects of their company. It's a commitment and anything less won't cut it. We have our eyes on the sky looking for a north star by which a company can plot the course for almost every business objective it has.

I have worked decades in the marketing industry, but even I don't walk into a client's conference room, have a one-hour chat, and then dramatically propose the north star of a brand. It takes time and consideration to build a brand with longevity potential that is still a natural fit for the established business.

I take my team, we do our research, and we brainstorm every potential brand direction for a client based on its ability to perform and inspire. Only the best of the best ideas that make it through the gauntlet earn the right to become a brand that permeates and inspires an entire organization. The brand, in turn, becomes the catalyst for developing the brand toolbox we've discussed here. Nothing less than a strategic arsenal of tools that can be pulled off of the shelf to help any client reimagine and reshape every topiary, tree, and flower bed in their company's "yard." There's a basic checklist of requirements that our agency puts all of our brand recommendations through *before* we believe it is ready to power your toolbox:

- Does the brand embody your company's "why" vs. your "what"?
    - *A good brand builds strong emotional connections.*
- Will the brand be a galvanizing force for your internal team?
    - *A good brand inspires teams to come together.*
- Does the brand differentiate you from competitors in an ownable way?
    - *A good brand is built off your business advantages.*
- Will the brand build irrational loyalty with your customers?
    - *A good brand takes customer loyalty to the next level.*
- Will the brand provide inspiration for how you will innovate?
    - *A good brand focuses your R&D.*

If any brand we are considering can answer "yes" to these questions, there is a strong possibility it could power the brand toolbox you've been looking for.

Getting Your Brand Over the Finish Line.

At this point, I think it should be worth mentioning that many of the most perfect brands to have sprung from our heads have never seen the light of day. In my opinion, this happens for two reasons: First, it is because agencies fail to demonstrate the full potential of their proposed brands to their clients. That begins with demonstrating you have a good grasp of the unique business objectives of your client. Without it, how do you know your proposed brand will have the level of impact you are touting? What's in a brand toolbox must change with every company's particular business needs. It all points back to where a company's opportunities for growth are. We start there and show our clients how the brand will ignite growth in those areas. My team and I have to be business analysts as well as marketing specialists because you can't pigeonhole a company's strategy, no matter how many agencies try to. The brand solution has to be tailored to serve the unique business objectives of each client. If a client cannot see that, they will not be blown away by your new brand proposal, no matter how brilliant it may be.

The second reason many great brand solutions die a horrible conference room death is that agencies fail to bring the brand to life in a way that their clients can feel its potential on a deep emotional level. It's a mistake to assume that because a client has a brilliant business mind, they naturally have the corollary artistic skills necessary to process how a brand will look and feel when it eventually comes to life. In fact, the opposite is usually true. I have found that the more brilliantly analytical a client turns out to be, the harder it is for them to successfully navigate a creative presentation. Without taking the necessary steps to ensure that they do, agencies should not be surprised when a great brand idea gets left on the table.

At this crucial stage, my agency will use every creative presentation tool at our disposal to ensure that a client gets goosebumps after seeing how their new brand will come to life. Whether it's video, photography, manifestos, sound effects, celebrity presenters, or even stand-up comedy, we know the stakes for us and, more importantly, for that client sitting across the table. So much is riding on putting the right brand with the right client. Whether you are an agency selling a brand to a client, or a CMO selling it to your president, or a CEO selling it to your board, don't think a great brand naturally sells itself. Be prepared to bring it to life!

With a brand powering your toolbox, you're on the right track to nourish and empower every department in your company.

Chapter eleven

Nourish
Your
Brand.

Or Else.

The road to brand glory is littered with roadkill. These are brands that have taken great care to get their brand exactly right and roll it off the assembly line, but then made the mistake of taking their eyes off of the road and following a wrong turn instead. Or even worse, they just stopped caring for their brand altogether and it sputtered to a halt. You must remember, a brand is a living entity that grows and strengthens with attention and dies from indifference.

You can't halfway commit to your brand. Otherwise, it'll barely take off before it's grounded again, and then all of your momentum will be lost. Business people think that the process of building a brand is the brand itself. But I'm here to say that although a brand has words infused with intention and possibilities, those words are limited. You have to infuse these words, an empty vessel, with actions that carry out the vision of your brand platform. It's the follow-through action that animates your brand with life.

Going through the process of building a brand with your clients, customers, and employees is an exciting endeavor that produces exciting results, and it's hard to resist popping the champagne and calling it a day. But don't fall under the delusion that this upfront work is the whole process. It is just the beginning of a long journey.

Brand building isn't some summer romance that you can toss aside after a few months of amorous attention. Building a brand means you are sharing a meaningful idea with the world that goes out and forges long-term relationships with real people. These people start to have expectations for your brand. In exchange for their attention and loyalty, they will expect your brand to give back in the form of information, inspiration, validation, entertainment, etc., whatever it is that you promise within your brand. If you take your customers' loyalty for granted and stop giving back to the relationship, your fans will start to feel disappointed, then ghosted . . . and may eventually turn into hostile, jilted ex-fans who are more than happy to sabotage your brand name across the digital landscape. Creating a brand relationship with the world is a hugely rewarding but precarious position to be in, so you have to juggle the moving pieces and keep your eyes on the road signs.

Your brand lives in a world that is mercurial and opinionated. Your brand must be fluid if it is to authentically respond and connect to the world it lives in.

When and Where to Nourish

When asked how our agency is uniquely different from others in the industry, we often say, "We nourish brands that nourish people's lives." The only way your brand is going to get out there and nourish people's lives is by putting your brand out in front of them. That is a belief we don't compromise on. And it shapes everything we do.

The Nourishment Cycle

Our alternative flywheel approach to the sales funnel. When Craveable Brands nourish their customers' cravings, their customers nourish the brand in return.

Strangers

ATTRACT

GROWTH

Prospects

Promoters

DELIGHT

ENGAGE

Customers

One of the fastest ways to reach your audience is with paid media, and for clients with budgets that can afford them, a robust paid media plan is part of our recommendation. But as we've discussed in earlier parts of the book, there are ways that your brand can reach your audience beyond paid media, such as PR, customer service, operations, in-store signage, and perhaps one of the greatest modern tools to empower challenger brands: social media.

One of the biggest inspirations for me in wanting to write this book was so that challenger brands of all sizes could effectively build and wield their brands to succeed against bigger companies with larger ad budgets. Before the rise of social media, that would have been a much harder feat to pull off for these brands. Our world today is centered around social media. People swipe as they stand in line for coffee and use it to fill the time. With the proliferation of social media, a targeted audience is within reach of any ambitious company. That means you have the potential to establish more touchpoints with your target audience . . . but only if you engage them in a unique way and in your own unique voice. Otherwise, you will be just one more swipe to be brushed aside.

What it takes to engage in a unique way will vary depending on your company and its brand. St. Jude's Hospital, a beautiful and amazing brand that I had the pleasure of partnering with, will likely find that inspired, uplifting content is the best way to communicate within its brand personality and will undoubtedly find wacky funny content to be inappropriate. Another brand like Geico strives to produce funny, unexpected content in line with their talking gecko. Regardless of your brand personality, social media can be *crucial* for small and medium-sized challenger brands to share their brands' unique voices and positions. If a brand is born from the true values and personality of a company, those values can and should inspire an endless supply of brand content for a company.

As you embark on the exciting journey of feeding your brand into the social media machine, one word of caution. While the majority of this chapter is meant to empower companies to commit to a steady stream of fresh brand content more often, there is a point of saturation you can reach with your audience that will produce a negative reaction. However excited you feel to share your newly polished brand with the world, be sure to release a "reasonable" amount of content. No more. Don't ever assume that your audience can't get enough of you. They most certainly can.

The frequency of your brand engagements will change depending on who you are, what you do, when you do it, and who you are doing it for. I have learned that some audiences can't hear often enough from their brand of choice. But those brands occupy rare air. The majority of brands need to monitor and gauge what level of brand engagement is appropriate for their particular audience. How often is your audience responding? How engaged are their responses? Is your following increasing or decreasing? These are all telltale signs of whether you are engaging often enough.

I believe it is better to test the boundaries with more content than less, and then pull back as needed. It's always better for a brand to stay top of mind. On average, two or three social posts a week is sufficient for growing brands. Yes, more often can set off the algorithms better, but that depends on the quality of your posts. Not all brand engagements are created equal. How often you choose to post online will also be dependent on an honest evaluation of what you're posting. Are your posts entertaining, informative, and fresh? Be honest with yourself. If you aren't, your customers will be. If you have a talent for creating great content quickly, then maybe you should be posting more often than those who don't. Also, if you do have the means to hire great content creators, then posting more often becomes more of an option. Most companies don't have the budget or time to produce enough truly engaging original content to maintain more than two or three times a week. The rule of thumb we follow is that half of your content should be original (and based on your specific brand and services) and the other half of your content can be shared content that has been produced by a third party but supports and extends your own company's values and brand. Your target audience should find the content valuable to them and appreciate you for bringing it to them.

There will be times when it makes sense for your brand to increase your brand exposure without the risk of wear-out. Stay alert for windows of opportunity throughout the year. Trending local or national news and events that your brand nicely intersects with can be a great time for your brand to stand out. Right now, it's fall in New England, and for many of our clients, that means it's pumpkin time! For New England Coffee, we've begun to ramp up their social media frequency to take advantage of the pumpkin frenzy. It would be a mistake to ignore the hype surrounding all things pumpkin-spice—coffee, muffins, scones—it's a clear niche within the coffee industry and a good reason to increase their frequency of posting. It's not a case of hopping on the bandwagon or following the status quo; yes, you need to differentiate yourself from your competitors, but you should still deliver what your customers want. And these days, it's pumpkin-spice *everything*. Are there times of the year when your brand's voice can resonate loudly? Plan accordingly.

Nourish from the Inside Out

Long-term success with a brand can only be a reality if your brand engages the two most important people: your employees and your customers. The people in your company are the living manifestation of your brand in the outside world. They are the ambassadors who deliver the brand experience directly to the front lines. If your own employees aren't the most enthusiastic storytellers of your brand, there will be a huge disconnect when your customers show up expecting a special brand experience and your employees' representation of your brand doesn't live up to theirs.

Making sure your customers and employees are on the same page means that you must make the internal company-wide adoption of your brand a priority before you share it with the world. At a minimum, launch both efforts simultaneously. Don't underserve this critical step. It is not only an opportunity to ensure an effective exchange of brand expectations between customer and company, but it is also a chance to re-establish your employees' commitment to their roles and your company. That means you have to create a brand that makes the whole company proud. Employees should walk through the doors and feel happy to be at work, committed to the tasks of the day. Granted, we can't show up like that every day; it's not some idyllic fairytale. But in general, if your brand elevates your employees from performing a job to fulfilling a mission, the nourishment of your brand will be enthusiastically shared by everyone.

With your brand bases covered, you then need a big ta-da. Reveal the new brand to your employees in a way they can feel it. This is no time for pie charts and long dissertations—this is a pep rally and you are the band leader. You are not asking them to robotically adopt a new company mandate; you are giving them a new reason to believe in your company and themselves!

Here is where you lead with your heart. By all means, share with them the strategic journey and business rationale that brought you to this new position, but bring your new brand to life for them in a story that positions your employees as the heroes. An enthusiastic workforce can be the determining factor for whether your new brand lives or dies. Find ways from the beginning to get them emotionally connected to your brand and then continue to find ways for them to communicate the brand to the customers, bringing it to life beyond the screens. Your company needs you to be an ambassador for "your brand" (and products), not your industry.

I always tell people that I'm less of "an ad guy" and more of a brand storyteller. Give your company a great story to tell over and over, and keep writing and evolving that story. You can't nourish a one-dimensional brand; I wouldn't even call that a brand! It's the human element that appeals to customers and by opening up that brand narrative, you'll forge a deeper connection with customers, one that can continue to evolve and weather market storms, and ride market opportunities.

Nourish Change

While maintaining a consistent brand over time is key, a brand must be flexible enough to evolve and support unexpected and inevitable changes in your business' solar system. How you choose to nourish your brand long-term will vary depending on a company's ambition, budget, internal alignment, timelines, innovation, etc. A company's brand and its business initiatives are meant to influence and lift one another. One cannot be successful without the other. Aligning these will empower your initiatives to hit harder and garner attention. As was mentioned earlier, it is important when establishing your brand to anticipate (as much as it is possible) the long-term forecast for your industry and how your company plans to navigate it successfully. These forecasts should be baked into the creation of your brand so that it is pre-built to flex and not break with those inevitable changes.

Companies that tie their brand too narrowly to their current business model run the risk of outgrowing their brand very quickly. Your brand should sit at 50,000 feet, not five. The best brands may feel a bit ambitious for a company at first. They should set a bar that is just a bit out of reach today but inspires where you're going tomorrow. At the time we created "America Runs on Dunkin'," Dunkin' predominantly existed in New England. How could they dare to stake claim to all of America? Was it too audacious? Maybe. But it was meant to capture the hearts and minds of blue-collar America, as well as be a geographical road map for their westward expansion plans that continue today. Brand and business are bound together beautifully.

Your new brand is going to be the inspiration for how you align your company and communicate to your employees and customers for years to come. If, out of the gate, you aren't clear about what your new brand stands for from both a rational business standpoint and an emotionally-driven one, then you're potentially creating a marriage made in hell. But when your brand embraces that duality of purpose and profits, you have created a growth machine that you will be able to nourish for decades to come.

To help illustrate this idea, think again of LEGO®. There will be times along the way when a brand creates such an appealing and magnetic brand that its customers and society at large will want to participate in nourishing it. This can happen in the form of user-generated content that customers build and further your brand, or it can be through word of mouth that spreads the goodness of your brand from one customer to another. In LEGO®'s case, its product has become ubiquitous with meaningful and memorable play. It's universal to look at the potential that sits in a pile of LEGO® blocks. Everyone has a different approach to building them, but whether it be a child holding up the colorful airplane they built for their parents or an adult posting the picture of the LEGO® Millenium Falcon they assembled, there is an inherent pride that results from the assembly process. This is the ideal place for a business to be.

I will caution you that your brand must remain present in those customer interactions. It is arrogant to assume that your brand is so fabulous that you no longer need to participate in how it is shaped. So keep an active eye and consistently support your brand's nourishment. LEGOLAND® resort opened in 1968, creating a space for parents and children to embrace that playful nature.[1] All the LEGO® video game tie-ins, from Star Wars to Harry Potter, allow fans of those properties to experience a playful and vibrant space virtually. Thoughtful and creative playtime has evolved from simple block stacking, creating a nourishing experience that is unique to LEGO®.

Nourishing a Relationship

A brand is not a human being that loves and can expect love in return. I know that sounds obvious and maybe a bit blasphemous for an ad guy, but it is true. Ultimately, we are participating in a transaction, an elevated transaction that is mutually beneficial and enjoyable to the customer and your company, but a transaction nonetheless. You have to respect the nature of the engagement you are involved in and respect your customers' time. Know when to engage and when to leave space for the brand to grow. You can't just make a child grow faster by constantly feeding them; the same goes for brands.

Nourishing requires you to feed the correct parts of your brand at the right time. It's not just a matter of frequent posting or large media buys. You can put out brand messaging that does nothing more than feature yourself and your products, but that's not nourishment. It is shameless product pimping. It is very easy to slip back into feeding a sales strategy that doesn't feed your brand. Think quality of engagements, not quantity of sales pitches.

Relationships are formed in the heart. Think about how you nurture relationships with your friends; after the initial introductions, mutual trust begins to grow and a relationship will start to move to more personal topics, like how you spend your days, what family means to you, and what you dream of being one day. In the same way relationships form in the real world, so too does a company's relationship with its customers. That is why in this world of brand building it is so important to be vigilant and respectful of how you're nourishing the brand's relationship with your customers. Customers are willing to let you into their world, and in many cases, let you represent them to the world. That is a very coveted and tenuous partnership that requires give and take. So respect the relationship by constantly nourishing a brand that nourishes your customers' lives.

Chapter twelve

Does This Brand Look Big on Me?

Look Big on Me?

You've done it. You built your brand and are nourishing it with all of the proper attention. It aligns with your values and has been integrated throughout your organization. But is it the *right* brand fit? Once you've put all this work into building something so personal to you, your company, your customers, and your employees, you need to gauge if the brand you've made is the perfect match for you and yours.

Great brands are not valued for their ability to rationalize their way into people's lives; they are valued for their ability to connect emotionally with them. A good litmus test is a simple question: "Is our brand creating buzz?" When a brand successfully connects with the world on a deeper, emotional level, people will talk. The key is making sure they're talking positively and constructively. They will talk to each other. They will talk to the press. They will talk on your social channels. Why? Because in sharing the great values that your brand embodies, they are sharing their own values with the world. They want people to make the connection between them and all the great things your brand embodies, so they share their feelings spontaneously and often. When those enthusiastic communications start bubbling to the surface, it's time to measure how honest that brand validation is.

Attached to Your Brand

The real brand champions will be the loudest because of their love of your brand. They are the ones brandishing your brand as a badge of honor for the whole world to see, becoming the walking billboards for your company. Your values align with theirs so closely that they can't help but latch onto everything your brand represents. These are the Harley-Davidson riders who have tattoos on their arms and patches on their jackets, or the country singers who tout their love of Yeti coolers full of Silver Bullets (Coors Light) by memorializing it into a song.

This is true brand attachment: the connection between a customer's sense of self and your brand. This bond is tapping into all of the memories and feelings that have built up over the years culminating in an easily accessible, positive self-identity. Maybe their dad had a Harley-Davidson motorcycle growing up, and now when they ride their Harley, they think of their dad—motorcycle rides, holding the flashlight as Dad pulls apart the engine, tagging along for the motorcycle meetups on the weekend. That tattoo isn't just about the motorcycle; it's the relationship with their parent. Or perhaps, in the deepest part of their soul, they see themselves as a rebel, even if they're a mild-mannered accountant by day.

The frequency of customer engagement can factor into their ability to incorporate your brand into their sense of identity. People who choose your brand every day, or on those special occasions that are most meaningful to them, are going to have more opportunities to build up that attachment. Brands can permeate all the way to core memories, but it comes down to being there at the right time and place. To build a relationship, or at least a more advanced one, you should measure your customers' frequency of use. This sense of attachment is what you're looking for when gauging if your brand is "right," compared to a general, indifferent attitude towards your brand.

Attachment implies a connection between customer and self, while attitude refers to a general judgment of your brand ranging from bad to good. Your marketing may come off as fun and exciting, and may even promote a positive attitude towards your brand. This doesn't add to a consumer's attachment with your brand though. Your brand should add value to your customers' lives, and as brand-related thoughts and feelings associated with everyday life tasks increase, so will their attachment.[1]

Not everyone uses brands as a means to show off their values though; these fans are just the loudest. There's nothing wrong with being the loudest, but it doesn't mean *all* of the fans of your brand are incorporating it into their self-identity.

Brand engagement in self-concept (BESC) is an overview of brands in relation to the self, and every customer sits in a different place on this scale. That relationship with a brand is unique to the customer and dependent on personal memories and preferences, and everyone will express this to varying degrees.[2] You may use Colgate toothpaste throughout your entire life, but that doesn't mean you're going to get a Colgate tattoo or post about brushing your teeth on your social media. Being someone's favorite brand is expressed in different ways.

Sometimes that expression isn't in how they interact with your brand but in how they interact with others. High-BESC customers tend to focus on their favorite brands but also keep their distance from brands they don't identify with.[2] Brands that don't fit in with their self-concept are seen as "others" and may draw ire in how they are talked about. When you're determining if that buzz around your brand is right, look at how people are talking about your competitors. Is there more frustration with competitors than your own brand? That strong attachment to your brand may be manifesting as negative attitudes toward your competitors; unfortunate for them, but a good sign for you.

The "America Runs on Dunkin'" campaign was empowering for middle-class workers who identified with Dunkin' Donuts, but also saw Starbucks as elitist. The High-BESC customers' fervor allowed all the political candidates at the time to promote imagery of themselves standing behind the working class just by being seen and photographed holding onto a cup of Dunkin' coffee. Starbucks represented the highfalutin elites, even though more people in the US have access to a Starbucks than a Dunkin'.[3] It's what the brand stood for that tapped into people's self-concepts. Starbucks offered a "classy" coffee experience while Dunkin' fueled the real "do-ers" in the country who weren't afraid to raise their voice.

The best way to monitor connections with customers' self-concepts is to be a part of that conversation. Online word of mouth has become a major indicator of consumer sentiments as social media offers a platform for the most outspoken brand ambassadors. Social media is an ongoing engagement though; the most effective social media presences are going to be built with frequent and responsive brand communications with consumers. Meaningful consumer brand communications are moving away from one-to-many methods such as advertising, and shifting towards one-to-one methods like direct messages on social media.[4] Customer journeys can move through platforms like Twitter, with direct tweets at a brand for customer service. Get feedback directly from the horse's mouth, and make sure to listen carefully or you'll squander opportunities to measure honest admittances of brand attachment. As data is collected and time passes, you'll be able to see the differences between brand attachment and brand attitudes.

Engage Your Employees

Your brand is not just engaging with customers, but your employees as well. It should be the "right fit" for everyone involved. While customer satisfaction is an important indicator of meaningful brand interactions, how your employees are bonding with your brand is key to getting a complete understanding. In fact, if everyone is doing their jobs better, your customers will be happier. If you find your customers aren't happy, employee engagement may be the issue. Reviews should be improving because your employees are associating with your brand and growing as brand ambassadors. What does the *right* brand look like for your employees? Have you set goals that align with your brand?

Defining your employee experience in relation to your branding is important early on for young companies and challenger brands. Your employee experience ultimately affects your customer's experience with your brand, so you can't waste time. With many brand interactions happening online, those rare human-to-human interactions hold even more power in the eyes of the consumer. These are the representatives of your brand's ideals and core values, and if they aren't able to execute service in line with those values, reviews and other data will help you to pinpoint where things are going wrong. Studies found that when customers encounter unfamiliar brands, frontline employees are critical in delivering service that supports a brand's identity. When this succeeds, unfamiliar brands have the potential to even surpass market leaders in overall brand evaluations.[5]

Ultimately, it begins with hiring. A standardized brand experience for employees as soon as they start working with you creates a unified brand experience for customers. That standardization process requires tweaking alongside your human resources and operations. The hiring process should be looking for employees who align with your brand's values and want to explore your brand's identity. It can't be a forced experience though; it requires an authentic drive for employees to provide a service or product that they can stand behind.

Robotic employees, who adhere to your brand mission but deliver it in a robotic fashion, are doing more harm than good. Employees should have some freedom within the limits of your brand for self-expression. That personal touch lets customers know that your brand's incorporation into self-identity is meaningful and may carry over for them. For challenger brands, it provides an assurance of authenticity in a sea of brands that can come off as cold and uncaring.

An authentic employee experience depends on how leadership is treating them. Employee retention is crucial, especially with brands that require frontline employees. If customers are engaging with a revolving door of employees, it's hard to develop a relationship with the brand. Retaining employees comes down to how they are treated and how the brand motivates them. In the end, employees are looking for meaningful work for a meaningful wage. If your leadership isn't abiding by your brand's values, then why should you expect your employees to abide by them? Their job becomes just a job. A transactional relationship with your brand will lead to unsatisfying experiences for everyone. A transformational leadership method, showing the benefits of the brand's value, has leaders acting as role models, living by the brand's values, showing how the brand will grow alongside and empower employees. If employees aren't happy with their own brand experience, take note and make changes.[6]

When we strive to create a Craveable Brand, we are constantly looking at how a brand can emotionally hook people and make them want to incorporate it into their own identities. It sounds almost dastardly, but I mean it in an earnest way. Our intention is to give people a product that is an expression of who they are; they can use it to celebrate themselves. Your brand is a living thing that has the freedom to change and inspire both employees and customers. If things don't feel right, do research, talk to customers, engage with employees, and tweak things a bit. Building your brand requires attentive listening and the ability to pivot in the moment. If you say things are "right" when they actually aren't, you don't have a brand. You have failure in the making.

Chapter **thirteen**

Avoiding the Brand Hereafter

The electric yellow font against a vibrant blue background used to signify one thing: Blockbuster. In many eyes, "Blockbuster sat atop the video rental industry . . . with thousands of retail locations, millions of customers, massive marketing budget, and efficient operations, it dominated the competition."[1] But while I can remember the Blockbuster, renting-movies-in-person days, its name is no longer mentioned in the entertainment landscape. Any reference to Blockbuster is in the form of a joke or warning: *You don't want to fail like Blockbuster, do you?*

It was *the* brand of the 80s and 90s. People would flock to the store to stock up on entertainment for family nights, dates, and casual viewings with friends—whatever the occasion, Blockbuster had a movie for you. Their brand signified community, comfort, and fun. Technically, the Blockbuster business lives on, but the brand has since died as the store numbers dwindled from the thousands down to one singular store left in Bend, Oregon.[2]

While Blockbuster was brought down by bankruptcy, many cite Netflix as the fall of this once-great giant. The initial Netflix model was delivery-by-mail, but it offered a saving grace: no late fees. On the contrary, the majority of Blockbuster's profit came from late fees.[1] Consumers surged to this new opportunity and Blockbuster's fate was sealed. It was unwilling to adapt to the trends and when digital streaming was later introduced in 2007, it wasn't long before the Blockbuster brand failed entirely.[3] When your profit model is built around penalizing your customers, it's hard to promote innovation if you are unwilling to adapt or change. All of this is to say that just because you have a brand and an established customer following doesn't mean it's time to sit back and eat popcorn.

I still remember the unequaled American experience that Blockbuster created for millions. The masses would excitedly walk down aisle after aisle in search of the perfect movie that would connect their posse for a brief moment of time. Blockbuster did that. And Blockbuster let it go. It failed to remember the "why" of its existence and pursued the "what" down a black hole of bankruptcy.

My agency had a front-row seat at the disastrous undoing of this once-great brand. While we never did work for them, we were invited in as part of a select group of agencies to help them turn around their death spiral. Our proposal, like many others, sought to convince them to expand their understanding of what their brand meant to the world. That Blockbuster represented something bigger to its customers than a retail experience—an experience that transcended its bricks and mortar stores. Sadly, our "radical" notion of building their brand around a tech-enabled universal movie experience was too much for them to bite off. As it turns out in the end, it cost them much, much more to cling to their outdated retail model. A great brand was lost that day. Cue the funeral dirge.

History tells us that if you've managed to establish a brand and secure audience attention, your work becomes maintaining your brand, feeding the relationship with your customers, and adapting your brand to the changing times and attitudes of your customers.

No one can predict the future. If we could, I'd be out of a job and going into business would be relatively risk-free. But you need to be the next best thing to being a psychic. Every decade brings new trends and inventions. Humanity is mercurial and fickle and that's what makes brand-building so crucial for businesses. You need to build a resilient brand that can weather storms and drastic cultural changes. Amidst all of the shifting around in our world, people still desperately look for comfort in stability and consistency. No matter the outer world, people will always love their families; they'll want a home; and they will seek validation and community. These are enduring values, and even with cultural changes, they are an underlying consistency. The best brands embody these universal truths and fiercely hang onto them. With a brand like this, you can bend and stay relevant to the market but still deliver your adaptability from a place of brand familiarity.

It's almost like a home makeover. The foundation of your house stays the same, but you may decide to update the furniture, change the colors around, and add some new decorations. It feels new and vibrant, but you still feel at home because the important parts of the space that are most comfortable and familiar to you haven't changed.

Keep Your Brand Relevant

The pressures are high and I've seen more than one CEO desperately trying every avenue to keep their brand alive. There are two elements for creating an enduring brand: **relevance** and **reach**. I've mentioned it before, but sometimes the hardest part for companies to pull off is nourishing their brand *after* they go through the process of finding it. You don't want to let all of that work go to waste! If you've done your homework and built a brand that is poised to elevate your company for decades to come, all you have to do is carefully steer it through those decades.

Keep your brand relevant to your business goals, industry, and customers. You don't want to be blindly dictating business decisions but instead, apply your brand in conjunction with all of those business factors to lead to a more compelling solution. On top of that, remain relevant to your audience by following culture and exploring how it shapes people's opinions and emotions. Be sensitive to what your audience is going through. These pain points will change radically over the years, but great brands manage the way they communicate their brands to be sensitive to those changes, ensuring they are connecting appropriately.

Culture, social, & economic trends favor Craveable Brands

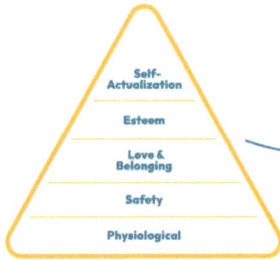

Self-Actualization

Esteem

Love & Belonging

Safety

Physiological

Our individual and societal needs have shifted

We're in the midst of a 'loneliness epidemic'

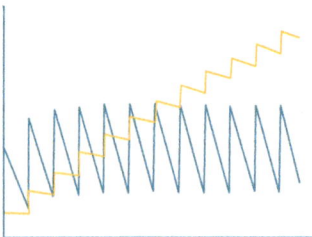

91%
of people believe in social's power to connect people.

Connection is the New Currency

It makes good business sense

Reach, as I talk about it here, is not about how many eyeballs see your efforts—that can easily be done with a bigger budget and still leave you wanting—rather, it's about reaching your audiences in a heartfelt and meaningful way. It's important to stay in touch with your customers. This means surveys, test groups, feedback, and anything else needed to curate some data and keep a pulse on your customer satisfaction. If you choose the easy route of viewing sales as the sole barometer of customer satisfaction, before long, you may be creating communication for an audience that will suddenly move on without any understanding of why. While current sales may be a good indicator of customer satisfaction today, they are not a guarantee of customer retention tomorrow. Always be aiming where your target is headed, not where they are at this moment.

Brand Euthanasia

Great brands can and will die. No business wants its brand to be banished six feet under, but it is the sad fate of even the most well-intentioned and diligent companies. A great brand can always be tweaked and adjusted as long as the voice and values remain consistent. There are some instances where a brand doesn't give you enough capacity to make the necessary changes; sometimes you're up against business or cultural shifts that your brand can no longer address. Or maybe you're faced with a business opportunity that your brand personality can't address or support. That's when you have to consider a brand shift.

In these rare instances, I recommend pulling off the bandaid quickly and essentially starting from scratch. You will of course want to still build off of your evergreen core values, and most likely your customer-recognized name, but the holistic brand approach may need a complete overhaul. It's always better to re-launch your brand than to have your brand misaligned with your values and product. Take Liberty Mutual: it used to be the serious face of responsibility on the insurance front. At some point, it became clear it was losing the battle to Geico's gecko and Progressive's Flo. Insurance, often an intimidating and stressful experience, was being approached with humor and Liberty wasn't playing that game. Their recent shift into a comedic approach has since been successful and, with their strong following in tow, Liberty was able to change its brand to keep up with competitors.

Consumers have a short memory; for that reason, I believe companies can adapt to the times and change their brand without creating too much disruption. It's almost like when someone you knew all of your life as overweight works hard to lose weight. It becomes the new norm, and a year later, you can't even remember them as big except when you see old photos. The same is true for brands. You get to know them as they are today and quickly forget the old version. Consider a parent favorite: the Jolly Green Giant. In the early 1930s, he was only referred to as the Green Giant and was a caveman sort of figure—gruff, unfriendly, and hunched over his bounty. This is a stark contrast to the current image of the friendly, impressive "Jolly" Green Giant who is proud to share his bounty with countless families nationwide.[4]

While this doesn't seem that drastic of a brand change, given that the green icon has existed for decades, it represented a necessary shift in the personality of the brand–one that the big man could use today. Engagement with the Jolly Green Giant as a brand now is extremely limited; he no longer appears in advertisements but is still used on product labels. Real diehard fans can visit the 55.5-foot Jolly Green Giant statue standing tall and proud in Blue Earth, Minnesota. Today, other than the nostalgia associated with the brand's icon, it doesn't stand for much of anything. It's a hollow vessel that remains emotionally dormant until it is either revived or slips deeper into brand irrelevance.

The saturation of the market, in every industry, has made it harder to stand alone and carve out space for your brand. If you *do* choose to rebrand, let the old one rest in peace and focus your energy on defining a brand that suits your company as it stands today *and* has the flexibility to shift in the coming decades. An inflexibility aimed at short-term goals will ultimately fail, even if you have short-term success. Burger King updated its old King character in 2004 with Crispin Porter & Bogusky, creating a memetic sensation with a giant plastic head. The viral King was often paired with scantily clad women in ads aimed at young men and had great success at the time.[5] The plastic-headed King, while great at creating buzz, was unable to produce a brand worth creating a relationship with outside of the targeted demographic. Burger King eventually dropped Crispin when it stopped seeing a return on the King character.

Even a fast food brand needs to be nourished with longevity in mind. A brand that reflects core values your customers can stand by will have a better chance than one that is insincere and shallow. If you feel your brand slipping through your fingers, take the time to reassess what your brand stands for and don't be afraid to make changes that may have an impact on your brand's future.

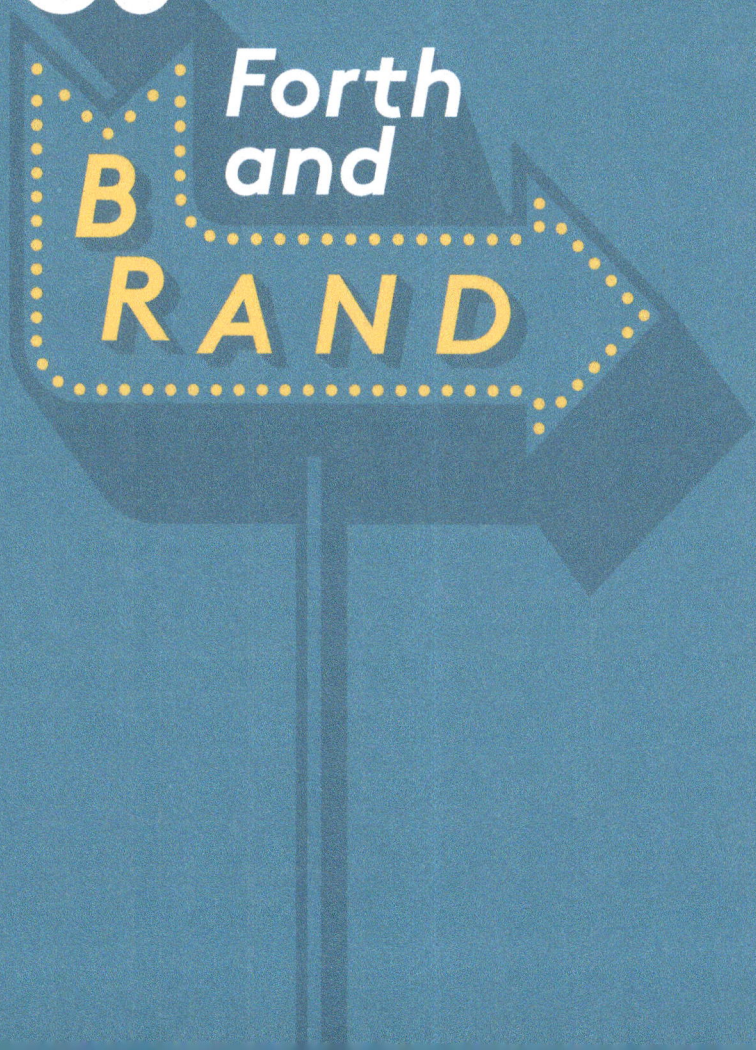

Go Forth and BRAND

Whatever your brand may be, whatever values you build it on, your brand will represent a story just by proxy of existing. At the end of the day, either you become the author of that story or others will author it for you. *Your* story is one building block of your brand, just as surely as your employees and logo are. Be intentional with your storytelling and nurture your brand beyond the pages of your employee handbook out into the world; let it affect every decision you make at the company. Every experience with your brand is another chapter in its story.

Many people don't know this, but James Patterson, the prolific author, was an ad guy before he became one of the world's best-selling authors. He was my boss at my first job at J. Walter Thomspon, one of the original iconic Madison Avenue Ad agencies. James Patterson likely doesn't remember who the hell I was because I was just a junior designer, but he played a small yet significant role in my brand-building career. I came from art school, a visual communication guy, and Patterson was the Chief Creative Officer of JWT. I interviewed with him and when I sat down to share my portfolio of speculative ad campaigns, he asked, "Tell me the story behind each of these campaigns." A reasonable question from a man who was to later become one of the world's bestselling authors and storytellers.

But at that time, I found his question off-base, if not a bit unsettling. Why? Because he wasn't asking me about the work and the campaigns in isolation, he was asking me to describe the story behind how I came up with each idea and the thinking behind why I thought it would connect with its intended audience. It doesn't sound that radical now, but for a fresh graduate, it upended my view of branding. Here I was a hungry ambitious marketing creative who until then was more interested in the craft of "making" and not its bigger role as a means of greater influence. It took me from thinking of marketing content as elements of a discrete ad campaign to thinking of them as chapters of a larger brand story that never ends—and that kernel of thinking led me down a decades-long path to honing the art of creating Craveable Brands. Your brand needs to stand for something deeply engaging, provide an irresistible product or service, and rally a craveable community. Only then will you move beyond lucky guesswork and flashy advertising with intermittent success to *real* branding that sustains growth over time.

A brand must become the holistic representation of your business and as such, it becomes the guidebook for every decision you make. A new product: does it fit your brand? Advertisements: do they embody your brand message and values? Hiring employees: do they resonate with your brand? It's a simple concept that takes time to weave into every fiber of your business, but it's crucial that you do; when you buy into your brand it will dramatically change your entire company. And believe me, you want this. There's more competition in the market than ever before, and unless you're devoted to your brand you're unlikely to survive the monsoon of market competitors.

If you need more examples of enduring brands, read *Built to Last* by Jim Collins and Jerry Porras. Researching companies founded around the late 1890s, they analyzed what made those brands last, how they've adapted to modern times, and what makes exceptional companies different from the masses. Even the longest-lasting brands had to start somewhere, and hopefully, you'll use this book to nourish your brand well into the future.

Challenger brands are the movers and shakers across all industries and yet they often get dismissed in favor of the big names. The key to success lies in taking a strong look at your brand, your core values, and yourself. Are you willing to grow alongside your customers and your employees? With a great brand in your grasp and a nourishing mindset, you have the opportunity to become a household name. You just have to *believe* you're not only big enough to brand but also big enough to build something meaningful and enduring. Trust me when I say that building a great brand that grows your company *and* inspires the world will turn your job into a passion—just as it has for me all these years. I wish you and your company exponential growth and happiness.

ENDNOTES

Intro

1. Simon Sinek, "How Great Leaders Inspire Action," TED Talks, March 4, 2014, video, 17:48, https://www.ted.com/talks/simon_sinek_how_great_leaders_inspire_action/c?language=en.

2. "Dunkin' Donuts History," Dunkin' Donuts, accessed February, 2023, https://news.dunkindonuts.com/internal_redirect/cms.ipressroom.com.s3.amazonaws.com/285/files/201610/Dunkin%27%20Donuts%20History_11%203%2016.pdf.

3. Kevin Moehlenkamp, "Dunkin' Donuts Outdoor Engine by Hill Holiday," April, 2006, https://adsspot.me/media/outdoor/dunkin-donuts-engine-2fd116f41294.

Chapter 1

1. Douglas Holt, "Cultural Innovation: The Secret to Building Breakthrough Businesses," *Harvard Business Review*, September–October, 2020, https://hbr.org/2020/09/cultural-innovation.

2. Kiera Sowery, "Emerging Trends for Fortune 500 Companies," *Startups Magazine,* https://startupsmagazine.co.uk/article-emerging-trends-fortune-500-companies.

3. "Fortune 500 Companies 2019: Who Made the List," *Fortune*, December 16, 2022, https://fortune.com/fortune500/2022/search/.

4. Ameer Drane, "Branding v.s. Marketing v.s. Advertising: What Are the Real Differences?" accessed June 6, 2023, https://www.eq-international.com/blog/branding-marketing-advertising-differences-versus-strategy-info.

Chapter 2

1. "2 Decades of Challenger Brands: What's Changed?" Contagious, January 9, 2020, https://www.contagious.com/news-and-views/how-challenger-brands-have-changed-20-years-after-eating-the-big-fish-adam-morgan-malcolm-devoy.

2. "Dunkin': The History of Donuts," DailyMail.com, September 25, 2018, https://www.dailymail.co.uk/news/fb-6208403/Dunkin-history-donuts.html.

3. "Advertising: Trying Harder," *Time*, July 24, 1964, https://content.time.com/time/subscriber/article/0,33009,939058,00.html.

4. "How to Win As a Challenger Brand," Kleber & Associates, accessed June 6, 2023, https://kleberandassociates.com/how-to-win-as-a-challenger-brand/.

5. "About Google,"Google, accessed June 2023, https://about.google/.

6. Winnie Hu, "Uber, Surging Outside Manhattan, Tops Taxis in New York City," *The New York Times*, October 12, 2017, https://www.nytimes.com/2017/10/12/nyregion/uber-taxis-new-york-city.html.

Chapter 4

1. John Leland, "How Loneliness Is Damaging Our Health," *The New York Times*, April 20, 2022, https://www.nytimes.com/2022/04/20/nyregion/loneliness-epidemic.html.

2. Kaitlin Menza, "How Biscoff Cookies Became the Snack We Crave on Planes," *Condé Nast Traveler*, March 23, 2020, https://www.cntraveler.com/story/how-biscoff-cookies-became-iconic-airplane-snack.

Chapter 5

1. Chidinma Nnamani, "Nostalgia Marketing and How Brands Recreate a Time from the Past," September 28, 2021, https://squareup.com/us/en/townsquare/nostalgia-marketing.

2. Valentin Saitarli, "Emotion: The Super Weapon of Marketing and Advertising," *Forbes*, November 4, 2019, https://www.forbes.com/sites/forbesagencycouncil/2019/11/04/emotion-the-super-weapon-of-marketing-and-advertising/?sh=5cc7583f4df0.

3. Peter Murray, "How Emotions Influence What We Buy: The Emotional Core of Consumer Decision-Making," February 26, 2013, https://www.psychologytoday.com/us/blog/inside-the-consumer-mind/201302/how-emotions-influence-what-we-buy.

Chapter 6

1. Maddy Chiffey, "Ben and Jerry's Mission Statement Explained: In-Depth Analysis," *Business Chronicler*, accessed June 6, 2023, https://businesschronicler.com/mission-and-values/ben-and-jerrys-mission-statement/.

2. "What Ben & Jerry's Can Teach Us About 'Irrational' Brand Loyalty," Rethink Retail, July 28, 2021, https://rethink.industries/article/what-ben-jerrys-can-teach-us-about-irrational-brand-loyalty/.

3. Jay Curley, "The 6P's of Brand Activism," November 19, 2019, https://www.linkedin.com/pulse/6ps-brand-activism-jay-curley/.

4. Jan Conway, "Unit Sales of the Leading Ice Cream Brands in the U.S. 2022," January 2, 2023, https://www.statista.com/statistics/755237/unit-sales-ice-cream-brands/#:~:text=With%20unit%20sales%20of%20approximately,410%20million%20units%20that%20year.

5. Erin McDonald, "Learn from the Masters: Why Apple's Branding Works," January 10, 2023, https://www.business2community.com/branding/learn-from-the-masters-why-apples-branding-works-02328187.

6. "Lego Overtakes Ferrari as the World's Most Powerful Brand," BrandFinance, February 17, 2015, https://brandfinance.com/press-releases/lego-overtakes-ferrari-as-the-worlds-most-powerful-brand.

7. "Our Purpose," KIRKBI, accessed June 6, 2023, https://www.kirkbi.com/about/purpose/.

8. "Construction Has to Change and Fast. Does LEGO Provide Some Inspiration?" Tata Steel, November 14, 2017, https://www.tatasteeleurope.com/construction/blogs-news/blogs/construction-has-to-change-and-fast-does-lego-provide-some-inspiration.

9. "Habitat's History," Habitat for Humanity, accessed June 6, 2023, https://www.habitat.org/about/history.

10. "Habitat Humanitarians: The Carters," Habitat for Humanity, accessed June 6, 2023, https://www.habitat.org/stories/habitat-humanitarians-carters.

11. "Celebrities Partner with Habitat to Reflect on What Home Should Be," Habitat for Humanity, accessed June 6, 2023, https://www.habitat.org/what-home-is.

Chapter 7

1. "Kenny Chesney: Get Along Lyrics," Lyrics.com, accessed June 6, 2023, https://www.lyrics.com/lyric/34967703/Kenny+Chesney/Get+Along.

2. Alla Elfimova, "How Most Startups Evaluate Marketing Agencies (and Why This Method is Flawed," March 13, 2023, https://www.transcenddigital.com/blog/how-to-choose-the-right-marketing-agency-for-your-startup.

3. Niamh O, "10 Brands and Businesses That Got Their Marketing Horribly Wrong," April 15, 2021, https://www.topmba.com/mba-programs/specializations/marketing/10-brands-and-businesses-got-their-marketing-horribly-wrong.

4. Hilary George-Parkin, "Size, by the Numbers," June 5, 2018, https://www.racked.com/2018/6/5/17380662/size-numbers-average-woman-plus-market.

5. *Up*, directed by Pete Docter, 2009, United States.

6. Allison Aubrey, "This Is How Much Celebrities Get Paid to Endorse Soda and Unhealthy Food," June 7, 2016, https://www.npr.org/sections/thesalt/2016/06/07/481123646/this-is-how-much-celebrities-get-paid-to-endorse-soda-and-unhealthy-food.

Chapter 8

1. Mark Singer and Rory McCallum, "Creativity as a Force for Growth," January 24, 2023, https://www2.deloitte.com/us/en/insights/topics/marketing-and-sales-operations/global-marketing-trends/2023/creativity-to-solve-marketing-challenges.html.

2. Jean-Marie Dru, *Disruption*, Paris: Village Mondial, 1997.

Chapter 9

1. Yvon Chouinard, "Earth Is Now Our Only Shareholder," accessed June 6, 2023, https://www.patagonia.com/ownership/.

2. Will Burns, "The Important Difference between a Tagline and a Brand Idea," *Forbes*, October 30, 2018, https://www.forbes.com/sites/willburns/2018/10/30/the-important-difference-between-a-tagline-and-a-brand-idea/?sh=f32d195761af.

Chapter 10

1. Tessa Zuluaga, "How to Calculate Your Restuarant Turnover Rate," accessed June 6, 2023, https://pos.toasttab.com/blog/on-the-line/restaurant-turnover-rate.

2. Julie Tucker, "Creative Entrepreneurs: Employees Come First for Sir Richard Branson," accessed June 6, 2023, https://www.headspacegroup.co.uk/sir-richard-branson-employees-come-first/.

Chapter 11

1. James Spillane, "Four Timeless Brands: How They Evolved to Stay Relevant," July 26, 2022, https://www.business2community.com/brandviews/mainstreethost/4-timeless-brands-evolved-stay-relevant-01491037.

Chapter 12

1. C. Whan Park, et al., "Brand Attachment and Brand Attitude Strength: Conceptual and Empirical Differentiation of Two Critical Brand Equity Drivers," *Journal of Marketing* 74, no. 6 (2010): 1–17, http://www.jstor.org/stable/25764280.

2. David Sprott, Sandor Czellar, and Eric Spangenberg, "The Importance of a General Measure of Brand Engagement on Market Behavior: Development and Validation of a Scale," *Journal of Marketing Research* 46, no. 1 (2009): 92–104, http://www.jstor.org/stable/20618873.

3. "America's Favorite Coffee Chains—Starbucks and Dunkin'," ScrapeHero, May 25, 2021, https://www.scrapehero.com/starbucks-vs-dunkin-store-report/.

4. Kelly Hewett, et al., "Brand Buzz in the Echoverse," *Journal of Marketing* 80, no. 3 (2016): 1–24, http://www.jstor.org/stable/44134939.

5. Nancy J. Sirianni, et al., "Branded Service Encounters: Strategically Aligning Employee Behavior with the Brand Positioning," *Journal of Marketing* 77, no. 6 (2013): 108–23, http://www.jstor.org/stable/43784338.

6. Felicitas M. Morhart, Walter Herzog, and Torsten Tomczak, "Brand-Specific Leadership: Turning Employees into Brand Champions," *Journal of Marketing* 73, no. 5 (2009): 122–42, http://www.jstor.org/stable/20619050.

Chapter 13

1. Greg Satell, "A Look Back at Why Blockbuster Really Failed and Why It Didn't Have To," *Forbes*, September 5, 2014, https://www.forbes.com/sites/gregsatell/2014/09/05/a-look-back-at-why-blockbuster-really-failed-and-why-it-didnt-have-to/?sh=13705f921d64.

2. Cailey Rizzo, "The World's Largest Blockbuster Is Still Operating in Oregon—And You Can Visit," May 3, 2022, https://www.travelandleisure.com/trip-ideas/visit-blockbuster-bend-oregon.

3. Patrick Kariuki, "How and When Did Netlfix Start? A Brief History of the Company," February 14, 2023, https://www.makeuseof.com/how-when-netflix-start-brief-company-history/.

4. "Jolly Green Giant," Walker Art Center, 2023, https://walkerart.org/minnesotabydesign/objects/jolly-green-giant.

5. Seth Stevenson, "The King's Comeuppance," January 23, 2012, https://slate.com/business/2012/01/crispin-porter-bogusky-how-the-hot-ad-agency-fell-from-grace.html.

ACKNOWLEDGEMENTS

I would like to acknowledge a few important influences and inspirations who had a profound impact on my career and the stories contained within the pages of this book.

There is a saying that says every successful campaign has a thousand parents, and every unsuccessful one is an orphan. To all those brave clients, creatives, strategists, and executives who stood with me at the inception of some truly iconic brands, I thank you for allowing me to help bring your amazing insights, ideas, and brands to life. It is impossible to credit the countless partners who educated and inspired me to exceed the potential of a chicken farmer's son. Assume every brand story in this book had a brilliant supporting cast. And I say to all of them, our collaborations have been the honor and joy of my life.

Also, this book would have never made it beyond my very limited attention span without the persistent hand-holding and brilliant guidance of my publishers who always believed I had a story people would find valuable. Thank you, Scott and Emily—I hope you were right.